KIP ADDOTTA
Confessions of a Comedian
An Autobiography

© Copyright 2018 Beacon Publishing Group, Inc. All rights reserved. No portion of this book may be reproduced in whole or in part, by any means whatsoever, except for passages excerpted for the purposes of review, without the prior written permission of the publisher.

For information, or to order additional copies, please contact: Beacon Publishing Group, Inc.

P.O. Box 41573 Charleston, S.C. 29423

800.817.8480 | beaconpublishinggroup.com

Editor: Susan Hughes

Publisher's catalog available by request.

Printed in the USA.

This book is a bit disjointed, and why wouldn't it be? My life has been that way. I know no better way to tell my story of my life and my work.
- Kip

Table of Contents

Foreword by Amanda Cohan	
My Grandparents and Their Family in 1925	1
My Early Childhood	3
The Rockford Children's Home	7
My Aunt Eileen, Grandma, & Uncle Victor	10
St Mary's	12
My uncle Victor	16
Uncle Victor, Brooklyn, New York	17
Uncle Victor and Aunt Eileen	17
My cousin Joyce and other kids	18
My uncle Victor and aunt Eileen	19
Excerpt from my Act	21
A Cloistered Life	23
Kent Creek	25
Tapeworms	27
Nino's Coffee Shop	28
The Knights of Columbus Hall	30
My cousins & Myself	34
The Beatings	36
Dennis A. Ferraro, General Counsel	38
My Memories of Kip Addotta	38
Grandma and Uncle Victor	42
Donna Chicca Francesca Addotta Dies	44
Out on My Own	46
Mary Bennett	51
Mary and I on our wedding day	52
Our son, Victor	53
Mary and I with a friend	54
Mary and I arriving at a picnic	55
Swede Clark's Used Car Dealership	57
White Corvette	58
My boy Victor (4) and me (21)	60
My daughter & granddaughter	62
The Death of My Wife	63
A New Wife for Me and Mom for My Kids	67
Buddy Hackett	69
Hit 'Em Where They Ain't	71
Gramer and Adams	73
My Decision to Follow My Dream	75

Lynn and I before we moved to LA	76
Our Trip to Los Angeles	77
My first publicity photo	78
Schwab's Drug Store	83
The Real Kramer	85
My First Manager	91
Back to the Road	94
The Tonight Show	96
The Mob	98
Frank Sinatra	100
Hecklers	102
Back to Work	103
Other People I Have Worked With	106
My Kids	108
The Memphis Hilton	110
My Comedy Material	116
Photo taken to send to my agents	119
Women	121
Allen Nechy	123
Watch Your Six	126
The Spider and the Cricket	127
In Las Vega	128
William Henry Cosby Jr.	133
Going it Alone	134
Make Me Laugh	137
Portland OR. February 6, 1988	139
Cocaine	141
The Death of My Father	143
Live from Maximum Security	144
"Addotta Shoots from the Hip…"	147
To New Comics and Comedy Club Owners:	154
How to Seat a Showroom	156
Stage Lighting	158
Sound	160
Stage Craft	162
Don't Curse	164
Hecklers and the Rule of Three	166
Becoming a Comedy Pro	168
Plebs and Twerps	170
Dinny	171
In Conclusion	173

FOREWORD BY AMANDA COHAN

Before there were thousands of comics standing in front of brick walls wearing T-shirts and sports jackets, talking about their girlfriends and the difference between dogs and cats, trying desperately to fit in, there were just a few guys who went up and said funny stuff.

Kip Addotta is one of these pioneers of modern stand-up comedy, and his style has been mimicked for years. He started in 1972 alongside people like Steve Martin, Richard Pryor, and Redd Foxx, and recorded his first album, *I Hope I'm Not Out of Line*, in 1982.

The style of his act on that album is reflected in a generation of comedians or at least the ones who were making comedy albums in 1981 and weren't trying to be Robin Williams. Addotta combines observational humor with classic story jokes that build to a punch line. There is no artificial attitude in his act.

His crafted, almost poetic material and studied delivery are honed for maximum effect using his full vocal range to the extent that many lines quoted out of context just don't work. He also writes "jokes to go" that anyone can tell, jokes whose fame has surpassed Addotta's.

The most important thing about his vision is the show. By working with great showmen, Addotta learned that people are not paying for lectures and morals or to be put down although there is a school of comedy that takes this route, and audiences have learned to expect abuse. Addotta steers clear of that.

Addotta appeared on *The Tonight Show* thirty-two times and spent four years as one of the challengers on *Make Me Laugh*, the comedy game show.

All Addotta wants to be is funny. "Laughter is so valuable and so cleansing," he said. "It's enough for me to be a funny guy. I don't have to be the guy who wears the priest's outfit. He's the Italian comic. There's the Korean comic. There's the Jewish comic. Stop it already."

As more comics jumped on the crazy originality bandwagon, Addotta had to work to stay ahead of the trends. That forced him to move on to spaces and places where other comics didn't really want to be, places too uncomfortable for them. He had to go where others wouldn't follow him. "It's a survival thing," Addotta said.

One of these uncomfortable places is puns, whose mastery Addotta demonstrated on his 5:04 single, "Wet Dream," the longest stream of puns known to man. All of them about one thing: fish!

Addotta says he chose the title because he knew DJs would think they couldn't play it on the air but would take it home to listen to it themselves. Then they'd realize they could indeed give it airtime, and they did. It is still a morning radio standard years later. The follow-up in 1986, "Life in the Slaw Lane," was as successful and featured an equally lush garden of vegetable puns, earning Addotta a featured article in *People Magazine*.

Another uncomfortable place in which Addotta is at home is honesty. "As a comedian, I don't have to be correct. All I have to be is ridiculous and funny," he says. Most comedians' fear of honesty translates into a fear of the original and results in stock material and hack subjects and a general sameness among many stand-ups, even those who purport to have an opinion.

Addotta believes most new comics are afraid to take risks. "Do I write a joke and go out there with my little testicles all risen up into my body and try a joke and see if it works? Or do I do something that I've already heard someone get a laugh with? The second choice is too often the one chosen."

The second choice is what creates limited trends in comedy.

"Specialized and politically correct humor is boring," Addotta says. "It's as entertaining as being obscene just for shock value or being topical just to get the easy laugh of recognition. I still take chances. I still write material because there's something funny about everything."

Addotta has quietly sold millions of albums, and his stand-up persona has also evolved into a curmudgeon style that leaves his audiences laughing so hard that they're gasping for air.

"One evening a man laughed so hard that he died trying to catch his breath. The coroner said the man had aspirated in his mask and died of asphyxiation.

"That's when I learned that one must periodically rest an audience, so as not to cause any more fatalities. That night, I thought to myself, 'Well, I've already done an hour, and this is a show that these people will never forget,' so I simply left the stage and went back to the hotel. I was shaking all night long.

"I have been shot at three times during shows by men who were drunk or high and didn't like the fact that the woman they were with liked me. Stand-up comedy is a dangerous activity. Billy Crystal has experienced the same fate. The only time people believe me is when I'm lying to them."

Everything that follows is fact. Just the facts and nothing but the facts; there are no embellishments. So Help Me God!

MY GRANDPARENTS AND THEIR FAMILY IN 1925

My grandfather, Jasper Addotta, came to America from Sicily. Of course he came by boat which landed at Ellis Island. There was a paper sign pinned to his back that said "Kishwaukee St.," which, by the way, is the name of an Indian tribe, the Kishwaukee Tribe. This paper sign told the immigration people where he was supposed to go. You see, in those days, one had to already have a job in order to enter our country.

Kishwaukee Street was in Rockford, Illinois, where there were many furniture factories, and Jasper had a job at one of them. He worked at this factory for about two years, saving every penny he could so that after he won his citizenship, he could go back to Sicily to get my grandmother, Francesca Guida, marry her, and bring her to America.

During his two year absence from Sicily, Francesca Guida had been living in a convent. This was done so that she would have some protection from other men and the soldiers of Mussolini's army. Jasper, now an American citizen, got on another boat and sailed back to Sicily to our ancestral home, Partinico.

He arrived at the convent in the wee hours of the morning. He shouted out, "Francesca Guida" several times, and finally the Mother Superior appeared in a window high up near the top of the building.

"What do you want?" she yelled down to Addotta (which is actually an African name).

Jasper said, "I am here to get Francesca Guida!"

The Mother Superior closed the window and disappeared. About forty minutes later the large main doors of the convent opened, and there stood Francesca Guida with all of her belongings. The two of them got married and then got on another boat to go to America. This time, since Jasper was already an American citizen with a passport, they could go wherever they wanted. They went to Brooklyn, New York, set up a home, and began their family in a building on Dekalb Avenue. My grandparents lived in one of the apartments upstairs (the second upstairs apartment was rented by a comedian named Jimmy Durante), and their first child my Uncle Victor would, one day, run a beauty salon downstairs on the main floor.

It was a few years later that my grandfather Jasper moved his family back to Rockford, Illinois, to get his children away from the Mob. My Uncle Victor stayed in Brooklyn, where he was already connected to the Bonanno Crime Family.

When my Grandma announced the was moving her family to Rockford, the Joe Bonanno Crime Family offered her the position of Boss of their Rockford chapter. The service that she would perform for the Family was to recruit new soldiers from Sicily. More on this later.

My Early Childhood

I have always been interested in biographies. And I find it interesting how so many showbiz people have had disturbing childhoods. Maybe it's a quest for acceptance that brings us to it.

I was born on June 16th, in Rockford, Illinois, to Frank and Josephine Bucalo Addotta. Both were nineteen and of Sicilian decent. I already had a three-year-old half sister, Kathy, from my mother's previous marriage to an American fighter pilot who had been shot down and died in the Second World War.

My grandparents Jasper and Francesca Guida Addotta ran a small market just east of the Morgan Street Bridge in Rockford. The market had been owned by my great-grandfather, Vito, who was no longer around. They lived upstairs from the market, and we lived with them. I spent all of my days at the market.

My grandmother ran the store while my grandfather sat in the back watching. This was a very Sicilian thing. It's not that he was lazy; he acted as Security. He sat there with a 10-gauge shotgun across his lap and was ready and willing to use it. The women did all the work and the men would sit and watch.

I spent my time playing around the store and eating the red Concord grapes my great-grandfather had planted. They grew on a vine in the back of the store. My grandfather would make wine from these grapes every year. The market's cellar was often filled with large, gurgling vats of red wine.

Generally, the rest of my time was spent causing havoc around the store. For instance, we sold live chickens, because at that time there was no refrigeration. The chickens were kept in small, wood-framed "One Chicken" crates with chicken wire walls. I delighted in kicking the walls in and letting the chickens out. My grandfather was not amused and would give me gentle pats on my bottom to curb this behavior.

The market was not doing well, because larger grocery stores with refrigeration were coming into being. My grandparents eventually closed their store, and we moved to a red-brick, four-apartment flat. My grandfather got a job at the local foundry, and my grandmother made the home.

My grandmother was good at everything: she made lace curtains; she made spaghetti; she baked bread; she cleaned and polished everything. Our apartment was spic-and-span. It smelled of bleach. It smelled of tobacco and good food and furniture polish. It smelled of everything a home should smell of.

She did everything to make the home just that, a home. She would make enough spaghetti in one batch to last the whole year. The spaghetti would be hanging, drying all over the apartment. She would roll the spaghetti around long, thin wires with flour on them, so there would be a hole down the middle of the spaghetti when she pulled the wire out.

In his spare time, my Grandfather Jasper would make baskets. These baskets were about eighteen inches in diameter and six feet tall, with a loop on the top that you could hang on a hook. He made enough baskets to hang all the way around the perimeter of our back porch. They were beautiful, and I loved standing on the porch, looking at them. These baskets had a purpose; they were made for drying beans. My grandmother would fill them with fresh cannellini beans, and my grandfather would hoist them up and hang them on a hook. This was done in the middle of summer when it was warm. The beans would dry and become as hard as wood. Then they were used to make Pasta Fagiiolo (pasta with beans).

My grandfather worked in a foundry, which is a factory that produces metal castings. Metals are cast into shapes by melting them into a liquid, pouring the metal liquid into a mold, and removing the molded material or casting after the metal has cooled and solidified. The most common metals processed are aluminum and cast iron. However, other metals such as bronze, brass, steel, magnesium, and zinc are also used to produce castings in foundries. This environment was dangerous, because the process produced fine metal dust that floated around in the air. There were no face masks in those days, so foundry workers breathed in the metal particles in the same way coal miners inhaled coal dust into their lungs. Hence the term "Rocks in the Box", a condition that many foundry workers and coal miners would die of.

Our apartment had two bedrooms. My half-sister, father, and mother slept in one bedroom, and I slept in a crib in my grandparent's room. I remember having a recurring dream that I was falling down a stairwell. I always woke up before I hit bottom. This was difficult for me to understand, because at the time I had never seen a stairwell. I was seventeen months old. Reincarnation? Maybe.

I can still remember playing with Kathy in the loose cinders that had been laid down to make our driveway along the side of the building. Cinders were the remnants of the coal that had been burned in the furnace that heated my grandparent's home. We would make mounds and shapes from the cinders and also throw them at each other. This is the only memory of Kathy that I have from that time.

The only early memory I have of my mother is of her left breast and nipple, which was pink and pretty. I was eighteen months old. Soon after that, my mother took Kathy, who was also later abandoned, and left for parts unknown. I didn't know why she did this, since I was less than two years old when my mother flew the coop! Over her lifetime she did this three times, once with me, once with a second set of children, and yet again to a third set of children. I often muse that she probably did me a favor. Any woman who would abandon her child could not have made a good mommy!

Sometimes I surmise that the reason I was driven or led to the media and performance was because I wanted my mother to be able to find me. But she wasn't looking! Everyone else found me. A half-brother found me; two of my half-sisters found me. One of my half-sisters, Jill, found my mom in a place called Spring, Texas. Jill asked my mother, "Do you know where Kip was?" and my mother said to her, "Oh, I know where Kip is. He's on TV!" In the interim my mother passed away, so I never had the dubious pleasure of meeting her again.

My grandfather Jasper was a stoic man, and though I didn't know him well, I knew that he liked me. Every afternoon at about five thirty he would come home from the foundry. As he passed by the couch in the front room, where I would sit waiting for him, he would reach into his vest pocket, produce three cherries, and toss them over to me as he went by, without ever looking over at me or breaking his stride. He also taught me how to scratch my back without asking anyone to do it for me. He would back himself up to a doorframe and move back-and-forth to scratch his back. The next time I had an itch on my back, I did the same, mimicking his movements. What a man! And me? I was becoming a big boy by leaps and bounds.

Not long after that, he went somewhere because iron dust had filled his lungs, and I never saw him again. Every afternoon I would sit on the couch and wait, but he never came.

When I was three years old, I became a sort of mascot at the local fire station. It was about a block from our home, and I would walk to it almost every day, heading down the street past the little brown house that always smelled like burnt baked beans, I crossed an alley and there was the fire station.

The firemen there liked me and would let me hang around and watch. On one of these visits, I was standing in front of the station when the big door slid upward. I heard the engine of one of the fire trucks running, and it began to move toward me. The driver couldn't see me, because I was short and stood below his field of vision. As the huge vehicle moved forward, the lower side of its bumper struck my head. The next thing I knew, I was lying under the truck, looking up at the motor. The driver must have heard the *thump*, because he stopped the truck. My skull had been split and it was bleeding.

The firemen took me inside the firehouse, wrapped my head with a lot of gauze, and sent me home. There was no lawsuit or anything like that. My grandmother simply told me that I should be more careful. Those were different times indeed!

The next thing that happened really made me angry!

THE ROCKFORD CHILDREN'S HOME

Shortly after my Grandfather disappeared, and as my mother had left, my father put me into an orphanage, The Rockford Children's Home. I remember it like it was yesterday. I was aware of what was happening at the time, and I was only four years old! It's amazing how little children can be so aware of what's going on around them.

My time at the orphanage was pleasant. The food was good, and Miss Ratz, the head of the home, was nice to me. It was fun playing with the other children, and they gave me a real bed in which to sleep. I felt I was becoming a big boy. One of my special friends was a girl named Kathy, a paraplegic due to polio who lived up on the second floor. Kathy was a sweet girl who slept in a crib and I liked her. She was a pretty Irish girl, and I think she liked me too.

Every morning one of the women would come to my bed with a large porcelain pot full of hyperemic needles and one of them had my name on it. I was given a vitamin shot in my butt and then I would go to breakfast in the dining room. When I was finished eating, I would run upstairs to see Kathy.

One day, in one of the orphanage's second-floor sunrooms, I somehow taught myself how to tie my own shoes. I was quite proud of myself and pleased to obtain this little piece of independence. I strutted around for days.

My grandmother came to visit me every day. I never saw my father, who was still living with her. He was a master machinist. He would set dials here, and then set another dial there, yet another dial over there, push a button, and this machine, which must have been huge, would make a part on its own. And this was long before the days of computers! The entire process was mechanical.

My father didn't have to go to war, because his job was strategically important. He worked for Ekstrom Carlson's, in a factory that made weapons parts for the war effort. He had an unusual work schedule. He always worked the night shift from eleven p.m. to seven a.m. Then he went home and slept until three in the afternoon. I didn't accept this as an excuse for him not visiting me. He could have done so sometime between four p.m. and seven p.m. I had done the math in my little four-and-a-half-year-old head. He could have visited me if he wanted to. This made me sad and angry.

My grandmother was not at all happy with my circumstances and voiced her displeasure and embarrassment over what my father had done with me. She didn't mention it to me, but I found out later that she complained to my aunts about it. My father had discarded me, but there was nothing my grandmother could do about it. So, she bided her time. Eventually that time came.

One day, my father asked my grandmother if she would cosign a loan for him so that he could buy a 1949 Cadillac. She told him she would, but first she had to have his written consent to bring me home from the orphanage. Grandma said, "I'll raise Kip, don't you worry. I'll take care of him, but I want him out of there, and I want him here with me." My grandma was my savior. My freedom had been traded for a car because of her.

I swear this is true! When I was just over four years old, my fascination with cars began, because that's when my father swapped me for his 1949 Cadillac. At least I was traded for a nice car. Trust me, I made a note of this occurrence regarding my father.

My grandmother brought me home from the orphanage to a house that I had never seen before. It was a two-story, single-family home, and the second story had been converted into two small, furnished apartments, making the first floor rather haphazard. The front room, normally the living room, was used as a bedroom for my grandmother and me. The dining room was used as our living room, and the den, off the dining room, was used as my father's bedroom. Toward the back of the house were a medium-sized kitchen and a tiny half bath. I took all my showers in the basement, standing over a drain that had a shower nozzle rigged over the top of it.

When we entered the home for the first time, I spotted my old crib sitting in the front room. I stared at it for a while, knowing that this was going to be where I slept, and thinking that it was some sort of demotion. After all, I was a big boy now! I had been somewhere and learned a couple of things. I had slept in a real bed. I believed that sleeping in a crib was beneath my stature. I would sleep in that crib until I was nine years old, and I was more than tired of explaining it to my friends when they came over to visit. I was sure the whole neighborhood was gossiping about the nine-year-old boy who still slept in a crib.

My Aunt Eileen, Grandma, and Uncle Victor

My grandmother was all about God, Jesus, Mary, Joseph and the Catholic Church. We would go to Mass every morning, seven days a week. We would go twice on Thursdays for Mass in the morning and Benediction and The Stations Of The Cross in the evening. We would also kneel at the trunk in our front room (our bedroom) and say the Rosary every night. I didn't really mind going to church, so I took it in stride. After all, I was my grandmother's right-hand man! That was a position of some rank, even for a young boy like me.

Once a year, Grandma and I would get on a Greyhound bus and travel from Rockford, Illinois, to Holy Hill, Wisconsin. At Holy Hill there was a seminary where they had built an outdoor Stations of the Cross. The Stations of the Cross or Way of the Cross Via Crucis in Latin, also called the Via Dolorosa or Way of Sorrows or simply The Way is a series of artistic representations, often sculptural, depicting Christ carrying the cross to his crucifixion in the final hours or Passion of Jesus before he died. The devotions using that series to commemorate the Passion are completed by walking from station to station and kneeling at each one to say a prayer.

St Mary's

A terrible fate fell upon the horizon, something I had not been prepared for. After all, I was doing fine. Everything was going well. I was fulfilling every expectation in my world and felt no need for something called school. I had to go to school? Are you telling me that knowing how to tie my own shoes, knowing how to say the Rosary, the Our Father, the Hail Mary, and knowing how to find my way to and from church wasn't enough? Jesus, Mary, and Joseph! I was six years old, and I was being treated like a child. Crap!

For weeks before the dreaded day arrived, I was sick to my stomach with the thought of going to school, whatever that was. Then, the day I had been counting down to finally came.

My first day of school had come, and I don't mind telling you that I was apprehensive. It seemed to me like punishment for something I didn't know I'd done, some mysterious infraction. But what could it be? I had been doing all my chores without fail. I was helping around the house. I was doing dishes, polishing furniture, sweeping the porch and the stairs and all the sidewalks around the house. I was mowing the lawn. Whatever it was, it was a bum rap.

This outdoor Stations of the Cross was along a circular half-mile gravel path, and as I walked along beside Grandma, she would crawl on her hands and knees the entire distance, stopping at each station to pray. Her knees would bleed profusely. And when she was done, we would get on the bus back to Rockford. She did this penance for the poor souls in Purgatory, a place where souls pay for their sins before being allowed to enter Heaven.

I was happy living with my grandmother, and when not in church, I spent my time learning to clean the house, wash clothes, mow the grass, and iron. I did all the ironing for our family. My grandmother spent her time cooking. She made everything from scratch, her bread, spaghetti, spaghetti sauce, sausage, meatballs and pies.

One afternoon she was at the stove frying meatballs, and she didn't know it, but I was standing right behind her. She picked up the frying pan and turned to her right. As she did so, she bumped the bridge of my nose with the rim of the frying pan, and hot grease splashed over the edge of the pan and into both of my eyes. I had never felt such pain! My grandmother was hysterical, thinking that she had blinded me for life. I didn't see a doctor. Grandma put special holy oil drops in my eyes, and I spent two weeks on the couch until the pain finally began to go away.

Grandma woke me up at six a.m. as usual. I dressed myself, tied my own shoes, and then we began to walk. Strangely enough, we were walking in the same direction as we did when we went to church. We walked by the Dr. Pepper plant, not a bad soda but a little sweet for my taste. We walked past the Pontiac dealership, where I had my eye on a two-door hardtop. We passed Nino's Coffee Shop and made a right turn, and there she was: the church. St. Mary's! Is this what school is? I wondered.

I'd heard the sound of children coming from a building next door when we were at Mass, and I naturally thought it was another orphanage. I couldn't help but wonder if those children knew how to tie their own shoes.

After Mass Grandma and I entered the building next door and climbed up three flights of stairs to an office. The sign on the door read "The Principal." A lady came out to greet us.

"Well, hello, little boy," she said. I looked around to see who she was referring to. "I'm Sister Anastasia."

She was a tall, well-proportioned lady with a rather prominent mustache. I thought nothing of this, because my grandma also had a mustache. Sister Anastasia's skin was a pale, grayish-brown color, and she was wearing some sort of military-looking outfit with a black veil and a heavily starched little white brim. She wore a huge rosary around her waist and looked as if she were a high-ranking officer in some sort of penguin army.

Sister Anastasia had a somewhat detailed conversation with Grandma that must have been some sort of background on my capabilities and stature in my community. I was relieved that Grandma made no mention of my still sleeping in a crib. Then Sister Anastasia escorted us back down two flights of stairs to a room called the first grade. I was impressed that they were going to start me out on the top. I guess knowing how to tie my shoes, dress myself, and recite all the words to the Hail Mary and the Our Father had impressed the principal.

Another one of the penguin people came out of this first-grade room, and Sister Anastasia introduced us to Sister Mary Margaret. She too was tall, in uniform, and rather pretty; however, she was certainly not of a high rank and didn't have the slightest sign of a proper mustache.

Sister Mary Margaret welcomed me, placed the palm of her left hand on the nape of my neck, and gently swept me into a room full of children seated at tiny desks.

The room reeked of corduroy, Brill Cream, and lead pencils, with just a hint of vomit. I liked it! All of the little twerps were wearing the same outfit, white shirts and navy blue pants or skirts. I wanted one of those uniforms, and I got one! Oh yes! This thing called school was going to be good, and in no time at all, I would most likely be showing these kids how to tie their shoes!

As for it being the first and top grade, much to my chagrin, I soon learned that it was not the top class at all, only the first class of eight. I would be in school for eight years? That was more than a life sentence!

I enjoyed school. For the first time in my life I had friends. I learned about things and found out that I was great at drawing. Once we were asked to copy a drawing of a girl's face. Freehand. No tracing. When I turned my drawing in to Sister Dorthia, she snarled aloud and said, "I thought I told you, no tracing!"

The other kids jumped to my aide. "He didn't trace it, Sister. He did it freehand."

I puffed with pride at this recognition and concentrated on my drawing from then on. However, drawing was really the only thing at which I excelled. Although my handwriting and arithmetic were also pretty good, the rest of the work was boring to me. History, Geography, English, Civics and Catechism? Those subjects were for the other kids. I wanted to draw airplanes!

My grades were not very good, and when I had to bring my report card home I was terrified. I knew that when my dad saw it, it would mean another beating. Never once during my childhood did my father sit me down and have a talk with me. His solution to everything was a beating.

Had he simply talked to me about it, I would have improved, but that was not in the cards. Dads need to have conversations with their kids. It would have shown me that he cared. But he didn't care. He looked at me as an obligation. An inconvenient obligation. He was a monster! I would eventually stop seeking his approval. And most of the time I don't even think about him. However, I still keep his ashes in the kitchen closet. I can't bring myself to discard them. Maybe I simply enjoy having control over him for a change. Maybe someday I'll let go.

My father became more and more predatory. As time went on, he would beat me! Not spank me, mind you, beat me. These beatings came more and more often. I believe it was because I reminded him of my mother, who had disgraced him in the eyes of the family. In the Sicilian culture, if a man's wife left him, it was assumed that it was because he couldn't satisfy her in the bedroom. This, I believe, mortified him, and he hated having me around as a reminder of his assumed inadequacies.

MY UNCLE VICTOR

My grandmother knew very well that my father, Frank Addotta, "had shit in his veins," as she would say. So, for my protection, we got on a train and traveled from Rockford, Illinois, to Brooklyn, New York, to lay low at her other son's home. At Uncle Victor's, as it turned out, I got a reprieve or at least a break from school.

    We arrived after a three-day train ride. My Uncle Victor picked us up at Grand Central Station and drove us to his home in Brooklyn, at 180 Sterling Place and the intersection of Flatbush Avenue, I found out later that it was just three blocks away from the home of mobster Albert Anastasia, the head of Murder Inc.

UNCLE VICTOR, BROOKLYN, NEW YORK

UNCLE VICTOR AND AUNT EILEEN

My Uncle Victor was a dashing man with dark skin, black hair, and a pencil-thin mustache. He always dressed in fine clothes and drove fancy cars. Later I would find out that he was a "Made" member of the Bonanno crime family.

My Uncle Victor's apartment was what they called a Rail Road flat (because it was laid out like a railroad Pullman car) with a front room with a long hallway that ran back past a den, four bedrooms into the dining room, kitchen, and a maid's quarters and second bath in the back. It must have been the largest apartment in Brooklyn or maybe even the world! I liked staying at my Uncle Victor's home. I had my cousins Joyce, Ronny, and Dawn to play with, and we would sit on the front stoop all day long with other kids who would stop by to talk, kids with interesting accents.

MY COUSIN JOYCE AND OTHER KIDS ON OUR STOOP IN BROOKLYN

Then, out of nowhere, that school thing reared its ugly head yet again. My Aunt Eileen had mistakenly enrolled me in a school called P.S. 9. It was no St. Mary's, that's for sure. The teachers at P.S. 9 didn't even have uniforms and neither did the kids. How pitiful!

My cousin Joyce and I were the same age, and we would walk to school together every morning. The school was right across the street from a place called Prospect Park. The second grade at P.S. 9 was all right, but the teachers and the other kids weren't very smart. I knew this because they asked me to sharpen their pencils for them every day. I did this without saying anything, because it gave me a chance to show off for the girls, who seemed to like me a lot. It made me feel funny in my pants!

Every week our class would have an activity called Front and Center. All of us kids could go up to the front of the class and do or say something fun. My first time up, I played a lawyer questioning his witness. I said, "Where were you on the day of June sixteenth?" The irony of this was that June sixteenth is my birthday. This was my first foray into comedy. And I got a big laugh!

After a few months, my grandmother put me into a "real" school, St. Augustine's, where they had real uniformed teachers. These ladies wore a slightly different uniform with bigger headdresses.

At this time in my young life, I continued to experiment with my comedy. This caused a nun to wash my mouth out with soap on more than one occasion. My take on the mouth-washing incident was that I was a bit too hip for the room. I was seven years old.

MY UNCLE VICTOR AND AUNT EILEEN

My Uncle Victor, a hairdresser, had a beauty salon on Flatbush Avenue called Art Beauty, but it was a front for other activities. He also liked to have poker games at his home. These poker games would go on for three days, every two weeks. They went on twenty-four hours a day. He would supply the dealer, a buffet, and cots for the players to sleep on. He would play and take five percent of every pot.

The people who came to these poker games were interesting. Doctors, lawyers, businessmen, local street characters, and Mob guys including Joe Bonanno and his sons, and members of the Gambino crime family all attended my Uncle Victor's poker games! I can remember being bounced on their knees as they played. They all wore guns that I could feel through their clothing. There was even a lady! Dora Myers, who was the CEO of Helene Curtis Beauty Products, and her father would come to the games. When police raided my uncle's poker game, the game was moved to Dora Myers' home. When the police would raid her home, the game would return to my Uncle Victor's flat. I remember all of these events as if they happened yesterday.

During these three-day-long, seventy-two-hour poker games, I learned what cussing was. I would be in the bedroom with Grandma, and at all hours of the day and night I would hear men and women coming and going down the long hall. As they left, they would be saying, "rat cock sucker, rat cock knocker, rotten sons a bitches, bunch of assholes," and all manner of great things! At seven years of age, I had no idea what the words meant. However, I had a sense that I shouldn't say any of them in my second-grade class, because I never got used to the taste of soap.

One day my Grandma and I were walking up Flatbush Avenue and I asked her where Grandpa was. She told me that he had died. She somehow explained to me what that meant. I thought about it for a long time and said, "Grandma, are you going to die someday?"

She said, "Kip, everybody dies someday!" That evening, I cried all night, hugging my grandmother.

Grandma realized that she couldn't keep me around the influences in Brooklyn, and I guess things had cooled off back in Rockford, so we took the train home. I was sad and was still coming to grips with all the new things I'd learned. Being a big boy wasn't all it was cracked up to be.

My Grandmother found me funny. I would say something and she would roar with laughter. She would ask, "Where do you get these words?" I didn't know the answer. I did seem to have a vocabulary beyond my years. But I was a good listener and would, when allowed, sit and listen intently to the adults' conversations. This is how I learned to understand Sicilian and, of course, there was TV and radio.

Along the way, I picked up English words as well. When I learned a new word, and the meaning of it, I would use it in my own speech. People laughed at me. I guess it was funny to hear these words coming out of such a young child.

EXCERPT FROM MY ACT

"Words, ladies and gentlemen, words; I am a purveyor of words. You can't see them. You can't touch them. And yet they are the most powerful thing known to man. Words! I am a student of words. I've been studying words for fifty years. Every morning when I wake up, I walk over to the podium that I keep in my bedroom and look up a new word. Today's word was anchovy: a small fish that smells like a finger.

"Words can change your life. Words like 'I do' will change your life forever. Words like 'Bartender, I'll have another drink' have been known to change the course of history, cause black eyes, broken noses, and can bleed your wallet dry."

We got on another train in Brooklyn and traveled back to Rockford. I was melancholy about leaving Brooklyn. I would miss my cousins Ronnie, Joyce, and Dawn, even though I knew that they would visit Rockford every summer, as they always had.

I would also miss Bobby Martin, one of the kids on the stoop, who never seemed to be able to figure out that he shouldn't run out between two cars into the middle of the street. He was hit by cars seven times. The gang on the stoop and I were so used to this occurrence that we would laugh every time Bobby would be struck and hurled twenty or thirty feet into the air and land on the pavement. He must have had a tremendous talent for landing on cement, for every time he was hit he would lie on the pavement for a moment or two and then get up, dust himself off, and rejoin us on the stoop. I don't know where he is now, but Bobby must have had more broken bones than someone who had a lot of broken bones.

As the train got closer to Rockford, I began to suffer anxiety, because my father was there and that scared me. I knew he wouldn't be at the train station. He wouldn't extend that kind of courtesy. I knew that I would see him soon, and that weighed on me like an anvil. I felt, though, that as long as I was with Grandma, I was safe. I also knew that I wouldn't always be with Grandma. "He" would be there.

A Cloistered Life

When we arrived back in Rockford, I went back to a familiar routine. When Grandma brought me back to St. Mary's, thank God Sister Mary Margaret was still there! She said, "Kip, you've grown like a weed!" Ha! That was a good one. I had never heard that one before. "Grown like a weed." Hmmm, now that's funny. Sister Mary Margaret still had not grown a proper mustache, poor thing. I never mentioned it to her for fear she would be embarrassed.

My grandma was protective of me. She would only allow me off our home property for half of an hour each weekday. Saturdays were different. I was allowed to be off the property for two whole hours! That was a big deal for me, and I looked forward to it. It was a cloistered life, but this was the life that I knew. I was a happy kid. However, I was still sleeping in that damn crib.

I rebelled against my crib by doing horrible things to it. With my finger I wiped snot on it. My crib was covered from top to bottom with boogers. I would blow my nose on my finger and wipe it onto my crib. You could have removed all of the wood from my crib, and it would still be standing, a great structure of boogers. Given enough time, my crib could become a suspension bridge made of nothing but boogers. I would fart at it too! I never peed in it; my pee was too good for that crib. Besides, ammonia would do damage to all of my booger work.

Other than my crib, I was very clean. My grandma wanted me to be independent. She taught me everything I would need to know to take care of myself when I was really big. I knew how to do laundry, ironing, cleaning, and cooking. I knew more about taking care of myself than any of the other kids that went to St. Mary's.

Grandma and I were still going to church every day and twice on Thursdays. We were still saying the Rosary every afternoon, kneeling at Grandma's trunk.

I began taking classes to become an altar boy at my grandma's encouragement. I had to learn the Catechism, Latin, all Masses were said in Latin then and I had to learn all the parts of the ceremony and my role in it. This took months of work, but finally I passed my altar boy test and served my first Mass.

I must add that in all the time that I spent with priests never once did any of them make any inappropriate advances towards me!

My grandma was beside herself with excitement. I'll never forget the look on her face when she was kneeling in the church while I was serving my first Mass. After a while, I learned the ropes and found out about the perks of being an altar boy. Holy Communion was served at Mass, and that meant wine was available. Fellow altar boy John Lynde and I would get plowed regularly and serve Mass looped. Altar boys can be naughty boys! There was nothing in the Bible that forbade it.

I learned a great trick. When the priest was serving Holy Communion, it was my job to follow close behind holding a silver tray under the chin of each person kneeling at the communion rail. I learned that if I slid my feet along the nylon that the altar was carpeted with, an electric charge would build up in my body. As I held the silver tray under the chins of the people, I would ever so gently touch their neck with the edge of the tray, causing a small electric shock to arc into their neck. I made believers out of them when I served Mass.

Sometimes my Grandma would go to a different church, St. Anthony's. On those days I would walk to St. Mary's alone. I remember the first time I opened up the church for seven o'clock mass. It was an eerie feeling, dark and quiet. I remember exploring St. Mary's basement and finding a back door leading to a grotto, climbing a spiral staircase to the bell tower. Thank God the door was locked. We used to put girls' books on the fire escape, one of our better ideas. I remember climbing up in the choir loft and trying to play the organ. Never did figure out how to turn the thing on. Someone once put black powder in the incense burner. We had a lot of stupid ideas.

KENT CREEK

Kent Creek was only one block from our home. I used to play there during my brief, half hour off the property each day. The water in Kent Creek was crystal-clear and about a foot deep.

Crystal-clear water means that wildlife can live in it. Things like crawdads, turtles, and leaches. I would catch these little critters and play with them. They were some of my best chums. I never harmed any of these creatures, because I liked them and I would play with them endlessly, catching them, holding them in the palm of my hand, looking into their eyes, and they into mine. Some of them were feisty little buggers like the crawdads and the leaches.

If I hadn't met a particular crawdad yet, they would pinch my hand with their little claws. But I didn't get mad at them, because I knew they were simply getting to know me. On the other hand, other crawdads that I knew quite well never pinched my palm and were quite comfortable there.

The most difficult of these creatures were the leaches. The leaches would attach themselves to my ankles and feet as I waded through the water. When I got out of the creek, there they would be, sucking my blood. I was neither afraid nor angry at this behavior. I would sit on the bank of Kent Creek and watch them for a little while. Then, I would take the very tip of their tails and gently peel them up and off my skin. It wasn't easy. These were determined little rascals. They were absolutely black in color, about two and a half inches long, and a half inch wide.

When I'd loosened their grip on my skin, I would hold them up and look into their eyes, though I don't really think they had any. Then I would lower them into the water and let them go.

There was a cement drainage pipe about eighteen inches in diameter, and if I was feeling especially adventurous, I would crawl up into the drainage pipe. It was scary. When I got about eighteen feet into the pipe, it was very dark, and every sound I made echoed around me. I would turn around and scurry out on my hands and knees toward to the light of day.

I was a regular visitor to Kent Creek, and when the Brooklyn wing of our family was in town we would have picnics there, where they had picnic tables and horseshoe pits. My Uncle Victor was good at everything he did, and there was no one who could beat him at horseshoes either.

My uncle Victor would also take my cousin Ronny and I hunting. We would go to farms and ask the owner if he wanted us to get rid of the pigeons from his barn. If he said yes we would throw a rock up into the barn loft and when the pigeons would fly out and we would shoot them, bring them home and pluck the feathers off and my grandma would dress them and roast them. I started feeling guilty about killing all these birds and never hunted again!

TAPEWORMS

You don't hear about them much today, but when I was a young boy, every once in a while, someone would get a tapeworm in their stomach. The tapeworm would attach itself to the lining of a stomach and eat all the food that one swallowed. The victim would get thinner, and the tapeworm would get bigger. Some people would use this as a method of dieting. They would swallow a capsule containing a tapeworm, and before long they would start becoming thin. However, this was not the case for my cousin Pamela, the daughter of my Aunt Mary. Pamela had somehow eaten tainted food.

I was staying with my Aunt Mary and my cousin Pamela, who is a couple of years older than I, for a week. The scuttlebutt was that my Pamela had a tapeworm, and my Aunt Mary knew how to get it out of her stomach.

Aunt Mary starved my Pamela for three days. She did not consume one morsel of food. The morning of the fourth day, as I was standing in the kitchen watching the two of them, my Aunt Mary fried up a steak with plenty of garlic. When it was suitably cooked, she cut off a bite and stuck it with a fork. Holding it up to my cousin Pamela's mouth, she instructed her daughter to breath in and out deeply. Pamela did what she was told. Suddenly she got the strangest look on her face, like she was about to throw up. My Aunt Mary instructed her to continue breathing in and out deeply, and Pamela did. All of a sudden, this white thing came out of her mouth and went for the piece of steak. When the creature attached itself to the steak, my Aunt Mary pulled it out of Pamela's stomach. It had to be more than two feet long. I had nightmares for weeks afterward, and from then on made sure that everything I ate was thoroughly cooked!

NINO'S COFFEE SHOP

When I was nine years old, my Grandma again would go to a different church, Saint Anthony's. On those days, I could walk to school by myself, although I never had the feeling that I was alone. I always had the feeling I was being watched and, indeed, I was.

I couldn't help but notice the olive-skinned young men with mustaches that I could see out of the periphery of my vision. They never spoke to me, nor I to them. I never acknowledged their presence but I was aware of them. More about these young men later.

On my way to school, I would always stop at Nino's Coffee Shop. I would walk into Nino's with a bit of a swagger. This was my turf!

If I didn't see Nino in the front, I would head for the kitchen, because that's where I knew he would be, making a huge pot of coffee. After filling the tank with water, he would put the coffee in the strainer with four or five eggshells and start the machine. I asked him once why he put eggshells in his coffee. He told me, "Because that takes the edge off the taste of the coffee."

After greeting Nino, I would take a booth all by myself. It was my booth. It was located near the front of the coffee shop, facing the kitchen, not the street. That's the way I liked it. I didn't have to order, because Nino knew what I wanted, and soon he would bring me a cup of black coffee and an order of toast. There I was, in my booth at Nino's Coffee Shop, with a cup of coffee and an order of toast. Like a normal person! No one else in my family came to Nino's. This was my coffee shop, my hangout, my place.

As I enjoyed my coffee and toast, I watched the other customers intently. Each of them was reading a paper, eating pancakes, or both. What fascinated me about these people was that they all had different methods of eating their pancakes and reading their papers. No two were alike. Each one dealt with his newspaper differently, folding it differently, snapping it differently, each in their own way. The same with the pancakes. They would take the fork and the knife and either cut them in a windowpane manner, or they would cut the stack into pie shapes with a crisscross motion, or a myriad of other techniques. To me this was the best spectator sport there was. I was fascinated by it. I was part of a group.

These were my cohorts, because all of us had one thing in common: we were all men having breakfast at Nino's. This is one of the most vivid memories of my life, and I cherish it to this day. They all knew me by name. I was Kip! And I knew their names too. They were all my buddies, at Nino's.

When I'd finished my coffee and my order of toast, I would stand up, reach into my right front pocket, retrieve the quarter that my grandma had given me and put it on the table with a snap. That's the way us guys did it! Then I would strut out of Nino's, take a right, walk half a block, turn right, and there before me, on the left side of the street, at the end of the block, was St. Mary's.

And where would I get this money? Our house was adjacent to a Piggly Wiggly warehouse and when tractor trailers would arrive to stock the warehouse with canned goods I would ask the driver if I could unload his truck for $6.00. If he said yes, he would sleep in his cab while I unloaded the whole of the trailer in about 3 hours. That was good money in those days!

THE KNIGHTS OF COLUMBUS HALL

The Knights of Columbus is a Catholic men's association with a great hall near St. Mary's. I'm sure that during the day, members would hang out there at the bar, have cocktails, discuss the day's affairs, politics, and upcoming events. It was rumored that the bishop and even the cardinal of the diocese would visit on occasion, for bonding, conversation, and, of course, cocktails. Nuns and ladies were not allowed. You see, the Knights of Columbus is a Catholic men's organization that is involved in charities. They also marched in parades, adorned in the Knights of Columbus black uniforms, red sashes, silver swords, and knight-like helmets, with great pomp and circumstance. They were beautiful, and we, as a diocese, were proud of them.

But on Friday nights they would be home with their families, and the Knights of Columbus hall would hold the Friday night Knights of Columbus dance for all the boys and girls of the diocese. On the second floor, they had a large, beautiful dance floor, stage, and side bar. It was free, so all of us boys and girls would show up. We were all about eleven or twelve years old. As you entered the hall, the girls would all be sitting on the left side and the boys on the right, facing each other like Napoleonic troops waiting to engage. It was like Napoleon on the right and Wellington on the left, and it would turn out to be the location of my Waterloo.

Mostly, the girls would dance with each other, and the boys would sit and watch. The music would be the Everly Brothers, Elvis Presley, Jerry Lee Lewis, and people like the feared Jerry Vale, Tony Martin, and Paul Anka, feared because they would introduce the dreaded slow dances.

During slow dances the girls wouldn't dance with each other. They would sit and stare across the floor at the boys, and we boys would sit there and stare back. The girls would gossip with each other, their hands over their mouths, and giggle. The boys sat in stoic terror, not talking to one another but knowing that someone, anyone, one of us was expected to be the first pitiful pawn to make the ultimate sacrifice and step onto and across the battlefield to engage the enemy.

On one of these occasions, as usual, I sat there with no intention of being the first to become the pitiful pawn splattered on the field of honor. I would wait for some other ill-prepared little Napoleonic sacrificial soldier to charge into the breach and confront Wellington's army, which was a seasoned, battle-hardened, well-equipped, and confident brigade with their crinolines and bobby sox and penny loafers and bows in their hair.

As I sat there waiting for one of our troops to march to his death, for some unknown reason, some ill-fated, unconscious impulse, I found myself standing. Then, with an unexpected urge, I stepped out onto the field. What was I doing? What had I done? As I took the second step, sweat beaded my scalp and poured down my face. I took the third step and found myself exposed before both Wellington's and my own troops, therefore committed to certain disaster. At this point, the sweat at the nape of my neck formed a stream, ran down my spine, through my butt crack, and formed a pool just beneath my young testicles, which had not yet dropped. I could feel the eyes of our brigade on my back. What was Kip doing? Has he gone mad? This is unprecedented! He has obviously lost his senses!

I was committed. In the middle of the void, my knees began to tremble; my legs began to fall behind the upper part of my body. They wanted to turn and run, but the upper part of my body knew they could not do that. My penis, being wiser than I, abandoned me, withdrew and disappeared into my body. Now I was alone. This would not be the last time the little laggard would desert me in the middle of an unfortunate, ill-fated, impotent skirmish. With all my strength, I moved my now-cramping legs forward, one after the other. But wait! What if I'm wrong? What if I don't fail? I'm a good person! I mean no harm. I'm doing my duty. I'm representing my brigade. This could work!

My eyes darted right and left, looking for an accepting face on one of these girls, someone who looked kind and forgiving. You never know. Some of them, one of them, might like me. My eyes focused, like a spring that had stopped quivering. There! That might be her. Cecilia Italis. She was nice; we got along. Granted, not the prettiest one, but this was no time to be fussy. Our eyes met, and the rest of her brigade, on either side of her, whipped their eyes to her, watching and scrutinizing my attempt. I found myself standing in front of her, and a small blob of feces fell from my butt and splashed into the pool of sweat that had formed beneath it. I could feel the eyes of everyone in the room watching, some 100 strong. There was a hushed silence. I forgot what I was going to say. Time stood still. The blob of feces had sunk to the bottom of the pool of sweat and was now resting on my briefs. That's okay; the odor wouldn't rise to anyone's nose. I had plenty of time. But what were those words? What were the words? Suddenly my mind retrieved them. I had the words! I knew the words! I gulped. I inhaled. I slowly pulled the hammer back, squeezed the trigger, and let them fly. There was complete and utter silence. My right ear could hear someone urinating a hundred feet away. Or was it me? I wasn't sure. Maybe this urine was pouring out of the bottom of my pant leg, onto my shoe!

"Would you like to dance?" She looked to the left. She looked to the right. She looked behind me at my troops, sitting at what now seemed a half a mile away. Her eyes scanned downward to the floor. I was sure she could see the urine dripping onto my shoe. Her eyes slowly came up and met mine. A second blob of poop joined the other at the bottom of the pool. Then she said it. It came out of her mouth as if it was an air raid siren. I'm sure the cars outside were stopping, and people were running and ducking and covering their heads for the impending bomb that was about to strike.

"Oh, that's okay!"

That's okay? What does that mean? Is that a yes or a no? That's okay? What was she talking about? What was okay? Am I okay? Is it okay that we dance? What's okay?

From behind me, I heard it, my own troops! "Uh-oooooh." Mutter, mutter. I had failed! That's what "oh, that's okay" meant! At the same instant, all of her troops crossed their legs in the opposite direction and looked the other way. I turned and traveled back across the field to join my now disappointed regiment. Closer and closer I came, approaching their stone-like faces. I had let them down. I had failed. The poop, now liquified by the sweat, was running down my inner thighs. I could smell it myself. I turned right. I ran to the stairs and down, out into the street. The liquified poop was now entering the top of my socks.

I ran all the way home, up on the porch, into my house, and closed the door behind me. I knew that I could never return to St. Mary's. I would have to find another school, a school where no one knew me. I peeled off my clothing, rolled it all up, and put it into the bottom drawer of the bureau. By morning it would be dry, and I could burn it all, along with the memory and the horror that had become my Waterloo!

The next morning, my grandma vetoed my intentions and told me I had to go back to St. Mary's. I walked all the way there with a pout on my face and was in a terrible mood at Nino's, but I still had coffee.

MY COUSINS DAWN, RONNY, MYSELF, JOYCE, AND PAMELA

My father, Frank, had a good side. He would teach me things. By this time in his life he had gotten into buying apartment buildings, and he maintained them himself.

He would take me with him to help, which usually meant that I would hold the flashlight. To this day, I'm the best flashlight holder that I know, bar none. I can hold a flashlight on point, while standing on a skateboard or perched on a basketball. He would introduce me to people as "The Boss." That was a laugh. I was just a little boy!

My father taught me about electricity, plumbing, carpentry, tree trimming, and all the other disciplines involved in building maintenance, and he taught me how to paint walls. I know these things, but to this day I don't know how to throw a football or catch a baseball. One of the buildings he owned was a former old-age home that he converted into living quarters for single women (wink, wink; nudge, nudge). It had three floors, a public area, a recreation room, a dining room, and a large professional kitchen. It also had forty single rooms and four shared bathrooms. I know, because I painted every one of these rooms. I painted the interiors of four buildings on a regular basis. I also mowed the lawns on every property, including our own. I was eleven years old. And, of course, there was no pay. Slave labor!

Very rarely, my father would take me to a movie or read the funny papers to me. I was so elated that he wasn't beating on me that I would laugh uncontrollably while rolling on the floor. Don't get me wrong, my father was an excellent reader and would mimic the voice of every cartoon character. He was also an excellent harmonica player and great on the xylophone, too. And, of course, he could dance. He had tremendous mood swings. Looking back, I believe that he was suffering from Schizophrenia!

On Saturday nights I would watch my father dress. He allowed me to do this, though at other times he would not allow me to look at him. When he went dancing, he wore sharkskin, a form of rather shiny wool suits. My father was quite handsome, with an olive complexion and dark, wavy hair. I loved watching him dress. However, I was not allowed to look at my dad at the supper table. For instance, if I was sitting at the supper table and got caught staring at him, he would backhand me across the face so hard that I would be knocked backward off my chair and go sliding across the kitchen floor. My father also wouldn't allow me to use the word love. "There is no such thing as love," my father would say. If I did use the word, my father would backhand me.

The Beatings

As bad as this abuse was, and it was bad, it was nothing like the beatings I would get on "special occasions." I could never tell when they were coming.

If I did something like wake him up, or if he caught me playing with matches, he never did anything right away because of my grandmother. She would stand there with the broom, holding it in a protective stance and say, "Frank! No, no!"

Then on a Saturday soon after, he would put me in the car, and we would go for a ride. On these "special occasions," when he didn't want Grandma around, he would say, "Get in the car. We're going for a ride." Even though I was terrified of my father, I loved going on rides with him. He would joke with me and tickle me. We could have a wonderful time. But on "special rides," I would notice that we made certain turns and drove up certain roads. I then knew what was coming. I would begin to cry, and I'd beg him not to do this. He just stared forward and drove to "The Location." I would pee my pants.

Rockford was a factory town and a union town, and the factories were only open on weekdays. On weekends, they were deserted. There were vast sections of town with factory after factory after factory that went on, block after block after block. My father knew where he was taking me, to one of the factories not patrolled by watchmen or police. He would stop the car at a desolate spot where no one could see what he was doing.

He would get out of the car and would come around to my side, open the door, and pull me out, throwing me down on the tarmac. He then undid his belt slowly, as he gazed down on me with a menacing stare. As he eased his belt out of its loops, he said silly things like, "You lost my pliers, didn't you?"

"No, Daddy, I didn't lose your pliers."

He said, "My pliers are missing, and I always put my pliers back when I'm done with them. Where are my pliers?"

"I don't know, Daddy. I didn't use your pliers!"

As my cousin Ronny would joke "He would beat me like he didn't know me!" He would begin whipping me and screaming incoherently. This would go on for a good twenty minutes. My father would beat me with his belt on the covered areas of my body. He made welts, but my clothing prevented anyone from seeing the markings. When he had his fill, he would stand there looking into space and slowly slip his belt back into its loops. And as he buckled it, he would say something like, "A man needs to know where his pliers are." Then he would drag me back to the car, throw me into the passenger seat, get into the driver's side, and slap me across the face for good measure. Then he'd put his finger in my face and say, "If you tell anyone what happened here today, I'll kill you!"

The reason he said that was because of my uncles. My uncles Victor and John had warned my father that their people in Brooklyn had heard of his behavior. If he didn't stop it, they were going to stop him. So they'd put their finger in his face and told him, "You've got to leave Kip alone. Stop it! He wants to please you. Stop beating the kid." And when they were around, he didn't. He must have taken me on twenty-five "special rides" during my childhood, and I never told a soul. I've never forgiven him. I have eliminated him from my mind! When I dream of my father, it isn't my father I see. It's Kirk Douglas!

Dennis A. Ferraro, General Counsel

My Memories of Kip Addotta

Lesson #1. There is an aromatic green-leafed herb used by Italians and others to flavor food, and you can say its name the way Grandma Addotta taught Kip to do, with the accent on the last syllable: bahs zee lee cah basilica.

Lesson #2. If you are doing something that you value, some activity that makes you feel good, whole, etc., then do not let what you perceive as someone else's (or some group's or clique's) perception of that activity make you feel less good about what you're doing.

So how was I so lucky to meet Kip and learn these two valuable lessons? The first necessary circumstance was that I was, fortunately, born to Mary and Sereno Ferraro, who, at some time after my arrival in October of 1946, lived on the ten hundred block of West Jefferson in Rockford, Illinois.

I don't know when Kip, his father, Frank, and Grandma Addotta first moved to the house just across the street, but my first memory of him was at about seven or eight years old, when Kip, who was two years older, would come over to my house to play on the few occasions that he was allowed out of his yard. It was natural for him to gravitate in that direction. My house was a shortcut to State Street and the Piggly Wiggly where his Grandma would send him for groceries, Cacciatore's meat market, and the soda fountain drugstore in between. The Italian connection was also on my side, Ferraro's, Giambrone's, Chiodini's and my side of the street had more available kids.

Of course, he and I would also play in his backyard, which was nearly adjacent to the abandoned Rockford Furniture factory and just a jaunt from the hobo jungle, an acre or so of woods alongside the rail line that bordered Kent Creek. Many times Kip and I would climb up steel ladders onto the roof of the factory or stand on the side of the railroad trestle over the creek while trains sped along a foot from our precarious perch. Sometimes we would cross the creek to look for scraps of leather tossed out by the workers at Hess & Hopkins tannery. And Kent Creek itself was a marvelous adventure for us, as we dug out crawfish from its banks or tried to dam it up with tree limbs.

The second component of my schooling in minor herbal matters, and those more important to development of genuine character, was Kip's personality. He was older and bigger than me, but I could outfight him. Even though he was a tough competitor, I often made him say "I give," either in a headlock or a full nelson. However, he never stayed mad at me for beating him at this child's play, and he was always patient and kind to me.

Before relating how his friendship and kindness led to lesson number two, let me color my recall a basil shade of green. I remember a summer day when Kip and I were walking south on the west side of N. Avon Street, about a third of a block from the intersection with W. State Street. I was about ten years old. If we'd turned our heads to the left, we would have seen the neighborhood barber shop, owned and operated by two brothers who, quite appropriately were named Frank and John Barber.

We weren't interested in haircuts that day; instead, we were on our way to the West End Library, which was about six blocks west on State Street. We probably were going to supplement our journey with a stop at Thompkin's ice cream shop across from the library. However, before we even got to the corner of State and Avon, Kip called my attention to some abundant green plants someone had planted along the sidewalk. Picking a leaf or two for us to smell, he informed me that this was basil, and that Grandma Addotta used this in her cooking.

This fresh and wonderful smell was new to me. My father and mother's parents emigrated from northern Italy, and although I'm sure they must have used basil when cooking in our home, I think this fragrant herb was more prominent in Grandma Addotta's native regional kitchen either Siciliano or Napolitano. And as you can see, the scene of my first discovery lingers even now.After Kip graduated eighth grade from our St. Mary's Catholic School, I still while in 5th or 6th grade followed in his footsteps, and those of many of our schoolmates, in learning the ritual practice of serving as an altar boy. This entailed learning all of the altar boy responses in Latin to the priest's prayers, learning how to set out the priest's ceremonial vestments, learning all the rites of Benediction, Stations of the Cross, blessing of the throats on St. Blaise Day, weddings, funerals, baptisms, etc.

One summer morning, after returning from serving Mass as a new altar boy, I came upon Kip standing on his sidewalk next to his new motorbike. He asked what I was up to. For some reason maybe because of the general emphasis placed on being a tough guy in my circles, or maybe simply because of my own insecurity and desire to fit in and be accepted, especially by an older, cool guy with a motorbike I responded to his question by trying to make it seem like I thought being an altar boy was lame, not cool.

Kip saw right through this mask. He kindly chided me by telling me that he knew I liked my new job. He told me, in so many words, that I did not have to pretend otherwise just because I thought others might think it was "square," not cool.

That's the last childhood memory I have of Kip. My family moved out of the neighborhood a month or two later. It was not until reuniting with him as a member of his audience in Chicago years later that I saw him again.

Perhaps there are other traces that I might retrieve, but these are two that I offer now to my old chum Kip Addotta.

GRANDMA AND UNCLE VICTOR

My grandma was an associate of the Bonanno crime family. The service that she performed for the family was that she recruited young men, potential soldiers, from Sicily and sponsored them into the United States. Grandmother was ideal for this, because she was one of the rare mob people who could read and write in both English and Sicilian, and she had connections in Sicily who could recommend ideal young men.

She would put them up in our home in Rockford, Illinois, while they got their affairs in order and then send them on to Brooklyn. You may be thinking that women could not be "made" members, or Dons, of the Mob. This is not true. Many people believe that only full-blooded Sicilian males could be "Made." Again, not true! Many Jews were also members of the Mob, "Bugsy" Siegel and Meyer Lansky, for example. If you're a good moneymaker, or if you performed special services for the Mob, you could be "Made."

My cousin Chris Addotta went on to be an FBI agent, but before they gave him his badge, they informed him that he would have to change his name, which he did because the name Addotta was too closely connected to the Bonanno family. Chris is now retired and living west of the Mississippi. Uncle Victor, Chris's father, disowned his own son because he believed Chris' joining the FBI was a betrayal of the family. They never spoke again.

My grandma kept me away from my father as much as possible. When she had obligations or wasn't feeling well, I would stay with my aunts and uncles. These visits were always fun. We went swimming at Lake Geneva, Wisconsin, and we had picnics. I got to play with my cousins and didn't have to go to church. My aunts were especially fun. When they would come to our home for cookouts, we would all sit at the picnic table. I got to listen to them tell stories and make small talk. When one of my aunts would need to use the bathroom, the other three would stand just outside the door and sing songs so that no one could hear the aunt in the bathroom make any noises. They would sing, whistle, and laugh. I knew what they were doing, and I would laugh too. They would say, "What are you laughing at? Get out of here!" I loved those ladies. They usually spoke in Sicilian when I was around, not knowing I could understand most everything they said.

Donna Chicca Francesca Addotta Dies

In 1959, my grandma was back in Brooklyn at my Uncle Victor's, living her last days. When I heard that she had passed, I was devastated. The woman who had raised me, taught me to cook and to clean, to sweep the floor, getting all of the dust up by first putting the broom in the toilet to dampen the ends of it, the woman who cooked everything from scratch and made the worst pie crust I ever encountered, suitable for the soles of shoes, the first woman who I had ever truly loved, was gone.

I was resigned. The most important person in my life had finally gone to Heaven. My entire young life, she had groomed me to be a priest. Now, as much as I worshiped my grandmother, I could move forward. I will always love her and know that she is still watching over me.

There were several people in my family who reported sightings of Grandma well after her passing. They reported seeing her sitting in a chair, crying and whimpering. I don't know why, but I believe that she was disappointed, after all her work to serve God in every way. I felt that she was disappointed in God. That somehow God had not lived up to her expectations. I believe she had tremendous remorse.

Maybe her final reward wasn't the one she had expected. I believe that her reward was here on earth and that my behavior would have to be impeccable so that she would somehow receive her just deserts in Heaven. According to Catholic teachings, I have never committed a mortal sin. In order to commit a mortal sin, you must first know that it is a sin, then contemplate the sin, and finally commit the sin. I have never done these three things that are required to commit a mortal sin. However, looking back, I have done things that I am not proud of. I would go on to be unfaithful to my second wife and I will always have remorse about that. But I have done my best to be a good person, and I believe that my grandmother has now found peace.

Thank you, Grandma!

I believe that I will spend plenty of time in Purgatory. I have been a naughty boy. But someday I will rejoin Donna Chicca Francesca Addotta in Heaven. Ah!

OUT ON MY OWN

On the day of my grandmother's funeral, my life changed even more than I expected. Upon returning home from her service, my father said, "I want you out of my house. Get out!"

In ten minutes I had a brown paper bag packed with the few clothes I possessed and was walking down the street. I walked across Fair Grounds Park, where I had played many times, and a few blocks beyond, I saw the most beautiful house I had ever laid my eyes on.

It was a huge, white, wooden structure with a porch that ran around its entire perimeter. I don't know why, but I climbed its steps and rang the doorbell. A lady answered the door and said, "Well, good day, young man."

I was fifteen and don't know why I had the courage to do this, but I called it up from somewhere and said, "Would you happen to have a room to rent?"

She looked me up and down and said, "Why, yes, young man, we do."

She let me in, and I looked around. I saw oriental carpets, porcelain floor vases, expensive oil paintings, a concert grand piano, and antiques everywhere. To this day, I have never seen a home as grand. She introduced herself as Mrs. Sorenson and led me up an ornate staircase to the second floor, which was equally as beautiful. She opened the first door on the right, at the top of the stairs, and asked, "Will this do?" I looked in and there was a four-post canopy bed, oriental rugs, lace curtains, and wine-colored velvet drapes.

I swallowed the lump in my throat and said, "Yes, this will be great!" Mrs. Sorenson then walked me to the end of the hall and showed me the biggest and most beautiful bathroom I had ever, or would ever, see. She said that the only problem was that I would have to share it with her and her husband.

"That will be all right," I said. "How much will it cost?" I had thirty cents in my pocket.

"Well, how does forty dollars a month sound?" she said. I told her that I didn't have any money right then, and she said that it would be fine; I could pay as soon as I could.

I found out later that her husband and she had lost a son of about my age years earlier. I believe that, in fact, they did not have a room for rent at all. They were being kind to a young stray.

She said, "Wait right here," and went down stairs. When she returned, she handed me a key and left the room, closing the door behind her. I sat on the bed, astonished. Less than an hour earlier I was living with an ogre, and now I was in a warm, beautiful, home. I believe to this day that Grandma was watching over me. Other events in my life have confirmed this to me.

Then I thought I would need a radio. I stepped outside and walked over to State Street, the main street in town. I was walking along when I spotted an electronics store. I went in and looked around. In one of the cases I spotted a little cherrywood radio. It was beautiful! I asked the lady behind the counter how much it was. She took it out of the case and put it on the counter.

"Twenty dollars," she said. I told her that I didn't have any money and she said, "That's all right, young man. You can take it now and pay us when you can." I filled out a short form with my name and new address, and with my new radio in my hands, I walked back to my room. Once there, I plugged it in and tuned it to my favorite station, WLS, out of Chicago. I was in my glory!

I thought, now I would need a job. I stepped outside and boarded the first bus that came along. I gave the driver twenty cents and we were off. I had no idea where this bus was going, but I said a Hail Mary to myself and hoped for the best.

The bus took me to a place called Loves Park and made a stop in front of a drive-in restaurant called Steak and Shake. I liked the looks of this place. It was all black and white, made of ceramic tiles, and it gleamed in the sun. I walked in and met a man named Hughey Myers.

Hughey Myers was Ex-Navy. A tough, bad man built like a tree trunk. He also had a harelip. One night, Hughey was fishing at Rock Cut State Park with a nearly empty bottle of Jim Beam by his side. At about ten p.m. that night, a park ranger drove up and told Hughey that the park was closed, that he had to leave the property. Hughey informed the law officer that he wasn't bothering anyone and was not going to leave.

The park ranger said again, "The park is closed, sir. You'll have to leave."

Hughey got up, grabbed his logging chain, and approached the officer. I found out later that Hughey always carried a logging chain with him for self-defense. The officer pulled his service revolver out and warned Hughey that if he came any closer he would fire. Hughey kept on coming. The officer stopped Hughey with five .45 rounds to the chest. Eight months later, Hughey Myers was back at work. That's when I met him. I say again, Hughey Myers was one bad man!

"What can I do for you, kid?"

I said, "My name is Kip, and I'm looking for a job."

He looked me up and down and said, "You're hired, kid! What size are you?" I told him my size, and he brought me a white shirt, a pair of white pants, a black bow tie and a paper hat. "You can start tomorrow. Be here at four p.m. I'll take the cost of your uniform out of your pay." I walked back to my new home. It took me two hours. Within three and a half hours of leaving home, I had found a beautiful place to live, gotten a line of credit, and found a job. I couldn't believe it!

The next day, I walked back to Steak and Shake wearing my uniform, and I grabbed a free burger when I got there. I hadn't eaten in two days!

For seven days of work, eight hours a day, I was making seventy-five cents an hour, food included, and the food was great! We had burgers, shakes, chili, fries, eggs, and bacon. Who could ask for anything more? I was a carhop, and before long I was good at it. I was fast on my feet. We could handle forty cars on the lot, and one afternoon I was the only carhop who showed up. I handled the entire lot myself. Running like the wind with a tray balanced on my right hand, as I approached the vehicle I would use inertia to swing that tray around and hook it to their slightly raised driver's window. In those days, there were no paper or plastic cups. Steak and Shake only used real glass shake glasses, and I never dropped or spilled anything. I was the best they had!

Not all of our customers were nice. Every weekend a 1956 Chevy full of boys would pull in and park out at the end of the parking lot. They would taunt me with remarks like, "You're a queer! You're so skinny, and you look like a girl."

One night they pulled a trick on me. The driver hadn't backed his car all the way into his spot.

When I ran up to the driver's side door to take the order, he put his car in gear and backed up to place his left front tire squarely on top of my left foot. All the boys laughed and jeered.

On another night, I'd had enough! When the boys called me a queer, I said, "Hey, I don't know where you boys come from, but I've never seen any of you with a girl. I think you boys are sissies." With that, they piled out of their car and started beating me and kicking me. I was down on the ground, stabbing them in their legs with my lead pencil. The boys beat me for a long time before I heard the most wonderful sound, the sound of Hughey Myers dragging a logging chain across the black top.

Hughey began twirling his chain over his head and said, "You boys better let my man up!" When those punks saw Hughey and that logging chain, they jumped in their car and burned rubber as they sped from the parking lot. I never saw them again.

Hughey helped me up, put his arm around me, and said, "You got your ass kicked, man, but you got your licks in. I'm proud of you!" For the first time in my life, someone had called me a man. I loved Hughey Myers!

After about six months at the Sorenson's mansion, I got a room at a house just in back of the Sorenson's. This room was a little cheaper, and I was trying to save up for a car. I maintained a relationship with the Sorenson's family and even recommended them to my Uncle Victor. He stayed at their mansion many times when he was in town from Brooklyn.

Two men owned the home behind the Sorenson's, and they lived in the basement of the house. The basement was decorated in a Tiki style. It was interesting. They had a room for rent on the top floor, and although it was nowhere near as sumptuous as the Sorenson's, I took the room.

Two doors down from me was a Russian factory worker. I could smell his dirty socks as soon as I climbed the stairs to my room. He played the same record twenty-four hours a day. It was Elvis Presley's, "Are You Lonesome Tonight?" Over and over again. This man must have been very lonely! I don't know how I stood it.

During this time, I came down with a bad fever. My grandma used to give me two aspirins and hot orange juice, and I would go to bed and sweat the fever out, so that's what I did this time. In the middle of the night the door to my room opened, and someone (I think it was one of my landlords) came tiptoeing across my room to my bed. By this time, my fever had broken. I leapt from the bed, grabbed him by his belt and the nape of his collar, and literally threw him down the stairs. I listened to him fall down three flights of stairs, and it sounded like he ended up all the way down on the Tiki level. I had to get out of there!

One afternoon, I was walking along the Rock River toward Steak and Shake, when I saw a beautiful home right on the river. I knocked on the door of this house and was greeted by a pretty lady. I asked if she had a room for rent. She looked me up and down and said, "Yes, we have a room for rent." Then she took me upstairs to show me a beautiful room which was overlooking the water. It was forty dollars a month, and I took it. Once again, I do not believe that this lady had a room for rent, but that she had taken pity on me. It was beautiful, and I felt more secure there.

I would continue at Steak and Shake for quite a while. It was my work place, social center, and school. I will never forget the wonderful characters I encountered there, and I pray for their souls every day. Wow! I was a lucky boy!

There were times when, for one reason or another, I had no place to live. So I figured out a way to get around it. Late at night I would go to a laundromat, get in a clothes dryer, and go to sleep with the dryer door slightly open. I knew that if someone came over and opened the door to put some clothes in they would see me, so I was safe. It was warm and cozy because they were gas dryers, and there was a pilot light. I would roll up my jacket and put it on one of the tumblers, so I would have a place to rest my head. To this day I look back on those times with fondness, and sometimes I'm tempted to pull into a laundromat and have a good night's sleep.

MARY BENNETT

I was working one night at Steak and Shake when a black 1958 Chevrolet sedan pulled up to the building. There was a mature lady behind the wheel and a pretty, young girl on the passenger side. The young girl gave me the most beautiful smile I had ever seen. I asked them if they wanted anything and they said no, but the pretty young girl kept smiling at me. After about ten minutes, they drove off.

This happened every few days for a while. On one of these visits, I asked them if they would like anything, and they said that they would like two sodas. I brought them their sodas and they tipped me well. Then the young girl started a conversation. She told me her name was Mary Bennett and that the lady behind the wheel was her mother, Maxine Bennett. You see, Mary was still in high school and wasn't old enough to drive yet. She asked me if I liked working at Steak and Shake, and I told her that I did, very much.

She informed me that she also worked at Steak and Shake on weekends during the day. I hadn't seen her, but obviously she had seen me, and I think she wanted her mother to meet me. Maxine seemed to like me. Mary and I began dating. I soon realized that Mary brought her mother along to see if Maxine approved of me, and indeed she did.

Mary and I went everywhere together. We were inseparable. Soon it was Mary and Kip this, and Mary and Kip that, to all the friends we had acquired.

Then I was invited out to her parents' farm for Sunday dinner. Mary had a large family, with two sisters and three brothers. Her father, Lester, was a mountain of a man, and I could tell he was not impressed with me at all. I wasn't his kind. He thought I was a city slicker. Imagine that. I was only sixteen, had hardly ever been out of the house, and he thought I was a city slicker. Maxine ran interference and stuck up for me and always would. I believe that she wanted something better for her daughter than being stuck on a farm. I think she saw an adventurous spirit in me.

Mary and I dated for two years, and I could tell that she was madly in love with me, and I with her. Her father never did take a shine to me, but he began to tolerate me more

MARY AND I ON OUR WEDDING DAY

In 1962, we were pregnant and got married in a beautiful Catholic church in Love's Park, Illinois. I was terrified.

How would I support a family? How would I feed a family? I was too young to be a father! I thought of running away and changing my name, but I realized that was a cowardly thing to do, and I couldn't do it. As the months passed, the fear did not subside. I was resigned to this fate that had fallen upon me. There was a knot in my stomach twenty-four hours a day. I had made a huge mistake. It was my fault. I wasn't thinking about Mary. I wasn't thinking about my new child. I was only thinking about myself. I was horrified.

OUR SON, VICTOR

Finally the day came. I got a phone call from Maxine, now my mother-in-law, informing me that Mary had given birth to a boy. When I went to the hospital I was shaking as I walked down the hall to the maternity ward. I stopped and looked into the window at the newborn babies on display. My eyes went from one to the next. Finally I came upon the basket with a little tag on it that said, "Boy, Addotta." I fell deeply in love with my first child. Suddenly all my worries seemed to evaporate. I went from horror and desperation to joy and pride at that very moment!

I decided to name my son Victor, after my Uncle Victor, and I decided to give him the middle name Michael, after the man who I knew would be his godfather, Michael Mangadegino, whose name, in Sicilian, means "Eat the grapes." You see, when he was in line at Ellis Island, waiting to enter the country, he was eating grapes. This happened to many immigrants when entering the U.S.

I turned and scurried up the hall to Mary's room. I gave her a big kiss and told her that he was beautiful. She looked at me as if I'd gone mad. I was so different from the husband who had been cowering for the previous months. She happily agreed with my name choices.

We moved into an apartment over a garage in Loves Park, Illinois, and set up house. We had nothing, but Mary's Maxine would see that we got everything we needed, including a bed and a few sticks of furniture. Soon, we had everything but money. During the winter we would sometimes run out of fuel oil for our furnace and would have to sleep in the kitchen with the oven door open. Mary's father was not going to support us with money.

He expected me to provide for my own family, and he was right. Somehow we got by with Maxine's help. She saw to it that our son had a crib and hand-me-down clothing she had saved from raising her children. Maxine was a saint, and I loved her. With great trepidation, I said farewell to Steak and Shake and all the wonderful people I'd met there: Earl Dewey, Hughey Meyers, Donny Taylor, truck drivers, and local businessmen. I needed a job with a more stable income. Little did I know that I would jump from the frying pan into the fire! Fire

MARY AND I WITH A FRIEND

MARY AND I ARRIVING AT A PICNIC

I found a job as a lackey at a cement company. The cement truck drivers were supposed to rinse out the inside of the cement drum at the end of each day, but they seldom did their job.

So they gave me the job of getting into the drum with a small jackhammer and chipping out the dried cement that the truck drivers were supposed to have rinsed out. Can you imagine the noise I endured and the dust that I was breathing with no ear plugs or face mask?

Inside the drum of a cement truck is an Archimedes' screw, which keeps the cement churning upward and doesn't allow it to solidify. The Archimedes' screw, also called the screw pump, is a tool historically used to transfer fluids from a low-lying level to a higher level. This screw, welded to the inside wall of the cement truck's drum, was razor-sharp from mixing cement, and the threads were eighteen inches in height. This is what is happening when you see a cement truck rolling down the road with the drum turning.

This was the worst job I've ever had, and it toughened me up for anything that might come along. Thankfully, I was smart enough to get out of there as soon as I could. My next job was drudgery, but compared to the cement company, it was child's play.

During that time, Mary and I had a friend, Mario, a young, handsome, Hispanic man who dressed impeccably and always drove a new Chevy Impala. We double-dated and always had a good time. One day, tragedy struck. Mario had been driving along, and as he sped down the highway, he got warm. He attempted to take his sports coat off and put it in the back seat. As he did this, his car drifted over into oncoming traffic, and he had a head-on collision and died. This was my first experience with losing someone my own age. To this day I'm uncomfortable with the death of Mario. He was a wonderful role model for me, and I've always missed him. This would not be the first time I would experience this sort of thing.

I've always had an obsession with cars, and why not? As I've said, it was a car that my father wanted my grandmother to cosign for that got me out of an orphanage. I acquired an old Buick Roadmaster convertible. It was the worst possible car for a young, broke father to have, and I began to rebuild it. It had hydraulic power windows, for Christ's sake! This was silly beyond words, but I worked my butt off on it and finally painted it with a spray can. Green! As I look back, it was a terrible car. I'm embarrassed that I bought it.

My father-in-law must have been livid with me, and rightfully so, for buying that car. However, my mother-in-law, Maxine, never said a word and continued to be my champion.

SWEDE CLARK'S USED CAR DEALERSHIP

Across the street from Steak and Shake was a used car dealership, Swede Clark's A1 Courtesy Motors. It was a Studebakers dealer, among other brands, but mostly he sold used cars.

I worked at Swede Clark's for about a year and a half. I washed cars, some fifty a day. I put the floor mats into the new Studebakers that came in.

There was a young man there, Tony Johnson, who was very funny. I would look up from my work, and this good-looking black man would be pretending to write on an imaginary pad, ostensibly to report my behavior to the boss. As he did this he would mumble, "Eh hum, yup, well that's the way it goes," and other accusatory sounds. He was very funny!

There was another young man who would show up regularly with wonderful little tools. He would remove the dashboard, revealing the odometer, and he would turn it back. He would turn back the mileage on cars as much as twenty-five thousand miles! This practice has evolved but not disappeared. Most people think that due to digital technology you can no longer turn the odometer back. This is untrue, and the practice continues to this day.

The schmoes believe that when they buy a car they should ask how many miles are on it. What they should be asking is for the service records on the car. The mileage of a car is irrelevant. Everything you want to know about the car will be in the service records. The service record will tell you what maintenance has been done, when it was done, and the mileage on the car when the maintenance was performed. It will tell you how many miles between oil changes, when the brakes were last repaired, the last time it was lubricated, and at what mileage, again, these services were performed. Even the lowest-priced car will go three million miles if maintained properly. The reason people trade cars in is not because they're worn out but because they're bored with them. The next owner of the car will be elated by his brand-new car because, for him, it is a brand-new vehicle! So the next time you're looking to buy a used car, stop asking for the mileage. Ask for the service records. If you're told that the service records are unavailable, turn on your heels and walk away.

One of my jobs at Swede Clark's A1 Courtesy Motors was to regroove tires. I would take a bald tire and, using a hot cutting bit, put crisscross grooves on the tire to make it look like it had some tread left on it. I was ordered to regroove the tires or I would lose my job, even though I knew what I was doing was wrong. I was only following orders!

WHITE CORVETTE

On a bitterly cold afternoon a few years later, when I was no longer working at the dealership, I was back browsing around the lot when I spotted a white Corvette. As you may know, Corvettes are fiberglass bolted onto a steel frame. Over the years and out in the sun, fiberglass fatigues. In cold weather, it becomes quite brittle. I wasn't planning on buying this car, but I asked a salesman if I could take it for a test drive. He said yes, and we were off. One mile down the road, the salesman told me to turn left into a gas station so he could put a couple of gallons in the tank. I did just that, and when I turned into the gas station, the Corvette's brakes went out! I rolled across the lot and hit a parked car at about twenty-five miles an hour. On impact, the Corvette shattered into little pieces, and there was dust covering both of us. There we were, sitting in two bucket seats, with no car around us. We looked at each other and broke up laughing.

The salesman called the dealership, and a car was sent to pick us up. When we got back to Swede Clark's, the showroom was alive with the news of what had happened. Swede Clark was standing there surrounded by a mob of at least thirteen salesmen. I was an onlooker outside the perimeter of this little mob. Swede Clark noticed my head bobbing up and down and said, "Can I help you, young man?" I told him that I was the one driving the Corvette. He said, "Well, how did you like it?"

I couldn't resist. I said, "Well, if you get those brakes fixed, I think we've got a deal!"

In 1962 I was working as a night foreman at Intercity Box and Plastics. We made boxes and plastic bottles. I enjoyed my time there, but I had other plans for my future.

I knew that I needed a trade and thought of my Uncle Victor, who always had beautiful cars and beautiful clothes. Not knowing that his beauty salon was a front for much more lucrative endeavors, I enrolled in The Rockford Beauty Academy.

I was also very shy so I took a weekly class on public speaking with Dale Carnegie. It helped me get over my fear of speaking to an audience.

MY BOY VICTOR (4) AND ME (21)

One day in 1962, at 7 a.m., I finished my shift at Intercity Box and Plastics and headed over to a saloon. I forget the name of the place. It was a big, dark place and had a large rectangular bar in the middle. Every stool was occupied by men who smelled of machine oil, tobacco, and whiskey. They were all talking about one thing or another, but you really couldn't hear what they were talking about, just the mutter of mumbled conversations between men who had just finished a night shift at one factory or another and had made a stop to toss back a couple before heading home. The sun was still low in the sky, and all one could see of these men were dark silhouettes.

The bartender didn't have to ask, "What'll you have?" because he only served one thing: a large glass of beer and a full shot glass of whiskey. When each man got his drinks, we would all do the same thing. We would take the shot glass full of whiskey and drop it in the glass of beer. As the shot glass sank in the beer, it would make a gurgling, bubbling sound as it descended to the bottom hence the name of the drink: boilermaker. It was a manly concoction, one that would settle ones nerves before having to go home to the wife.

I was only nineteen at the time and definitely the youngest and smallest one at the bar, so I kept to myself, knowing that these were rough customers who were tired and in no mood for wisecracks, something I seemed to have an endless supply of.

On one of these mornings, two men on the opposite side of the bar from me got into a row about something or other, got up from their barstools, and squared off in the middle of the floor. Their fists were clenched, and they were ready to rock and roll.

The bartender walked through an opening in the bar as if he had done it a thousand times before. Upon reaching the two men, he grabbed the larger of the two by the arms, from behind. I'm sure his intention was to stop the brawl before it got started. But the smaller of the two took advantage of this, grabbed a beer bottle, and whacked the larger man on the side of his head as hard as he could. The bottle didn't break but made a horrible sound when it connected with the man's temple, kind of like the sound a metal bat makes when it connects with a fast hardball.

The bartender loosened his grip, and the larger man slumped to the floor. No one at the bar looked up from their drink, and no one checked to see if the man was still alive. The bartender and the assailant simply dragged the body out the back door and left it in the parking lot. The bartender went back to his station behind the bar, and the police were never called. These were different times!

At that point, I paid my bill of fifty cents (!) and left. As I drove home, I believed that I had witnessed a killing, but I had no time for that. I had to get home and shower before going to The Rockford Beauty Academy. You see, I was studying, part time, to become a hairdresser.

I would work from eleven at night until seven in the morning. I would then go home, shower, change clothes, and be at beauty school from nine a.m. until two p.m. Then I would go home and sleep from three p.m. to nine p.m. This went on for nine months. I was constantly exhausted. Somehow I made it through, got my license, and began to work as a hairdresser. I got a job working at The May Company in their beauty salon. Not too long after I started, I was offered a job from the Martha Harper chain managing one of their salons. I worked at this profession for eight years.

I was a popular hairdresser and a good stylist. I had two other people working for me, and I did at least twenty-five people a day myself, one every thirty minutes. It was backbreaking work, and with all the hair spray in the air, it was not good for my health. It was going well, however, and I built up a good clientele, although in those days there wasn't much money in it. My wife, Mary, even came in and did manicures for the customers.

During this time, Mary and I were blessed with a girl, my daughter, Kathy, named after my sister Kathy, wherever she was. Just like her mother, Kathy was, and remains, a girl to be reckoned with. She is a woman who goes after life with great gusto. I not only love her; I have tremendous respect for her. She is now married to a wonderful man, Michael, and they have a daughter, my granddaughter.

MY DAUGHTER KATHY AND MY GRANDDAUGHTER KAYLA

The Death of My Wife

It was 1966 and Mary started looking bad. Her skin began to look more and more yellow. I asked her if she was using something, like a sort of lotion you put on to make it look like you're tanned. She was not. Mary was addicted to a very popular soft drink and drank three 24-bottle cases of it a week. I paid no attention to this. At that time we didn't know that this soft drink, taken to excess, would destroy one's kidneys. Mary was ill and diagnosed with kidney failure when I took her to the doctor. In addition to this, she had developed glomerulonephritis, otherwise known as blood clots in one's legs.

The treatment for clearing her blood of uric acid was a contraption called a dialysis machine. At that time there was only one in the entire state of Illinois. That machine was located in The Illinois Medical Health Center at The University of Illinois in Chicago. It was ninety miles away. I would travel with Mary to Chicago every three days for her treatment. No problem! I loved this girl, and, of course, taking her to Chicago every three days was my pleasure. Anything it took to keep her alive, I was more than happy to do.

Mary endured these dialysis treatments, hooked up to the machine for six hours at a time. Unfortunately, she continued to become weaker. She lost all of her muscle tone, and her arms and legs seemed hollow. This routine went on for six months. Mary's health further declined. I had to admit her to The Swedish American Hospital in Rockford, as she was in need of constant care.

I would go to see her every evening, and she would greet me with the most wonderful and frightened, "Hi." She was so glad to see me, but I heard the fear in her voice. We would hold hands and talk about our kids. I assured her that Victor and Kathy were safe at Les and Maxine's. Members of her family and my family would visit her during the day.

On one of my visits, her doctor pulled me aside to tell me that there was no hope that Mary would survive. I wasn't mature enough to really understand what he was saying. I honestly left the hospital wondering what he meant by that. I had just spoken with her. She was fine. Weak, yes, but I had no experience with someone dying. I had been very ill many, many times in my life, with high fevers and chills and shivering to the point of quaking my body, and I always survived. I naively assumed that she would get well. She was twenty-three years old! People don't die at twenty-three. Whatever that doctor meant, he certainly didn't know anything about Mary. If he had just given her three aspirins and hot orange juice she would have pulled out of it. That's what my grandmother did, and I always pulled out of it. Obviously that doctor didn't know what he was talking about. The next time I visited her, I brought her aspirins and orange juice, which I heated up and gave to her. Surely she would be all right in a few hours. She would sweat it out.

One day, my Aunts Eileen and Mary were in her room. The moment before "it" happened, Mary sat up in bed and said, "I feel great!" Then she died in my Aunt Eileen's arms. You see, a blood clot in her leg came loose, traveled through her arteries, and stopped her heart. In doing so, it forced blood to her brain, so she felt wonderful for a split second. When it got to her heart it stopped, and Mary was dead. She was twenty-three years old.

I went into shock. I couldn't believe my Mary was gone. She was a wonderful girl with many friends. Everyone loved her, and I didn't know what I was going to do without her.

I had the grim task of arranging for my wife's funeral, even though I had not actually gotten the fact that she was really going to die. I called St. Mary's and spoke with Father Crosby, asking him to perform the Last Rites. I had been an altar boy at St. Mary's and knew all the priests at that parish and had served Mass many times for each of them. Father Crosby asked me where we lived, and because we no longer were in their parish, they would not perform the rites. To my amazement and horror, they turned me down.

When I called St. Anthony's, a priest was sent over immediately. You see, my grandmother, Donna Chicca Francesca Addotta, was extremely active in that parish, my cousins were married in St. Anthony's, and the Addotta family was well known and respected there. The priests were mainly of Italian/Sicilian descent, so they were eager to help an Addotta in any way they could, especially one related to my grandmother. Grandma had come through for me again!

Soon after Mary's passing, the movie, *Love Story* came out. It's the story of a young couple in love, and the girl dies. The Four Seasons had a hit record titled "Bye Bye Baby." The chorus included the words, "Bye bye, baby, bye bye." To me it seemed that I was in the middle of a nightmare, and constantly, blow after blow, my heart was being broken again and again. As I am writing this, tears are streaming down my face, and this is not about me. It's about Mary! My heart was broken, and I took both of these reminders personally.

I called my father and told him the news and asked him to come to the funeral. He begged off by saying, "I never approved of Mary."

I said, "Dad, if you are not at Mary's funeral, you can forget that you have a son." He was not there.

I made Mary's funeral arrangements and was in a daze. How do I tell my children? I was guilt-ridden. I couldn't figure out why I wasn't crying. As I said, I was in shock. Finally, at her funeral, in the same church where we had been married, the tears came. It was awful.

After Mary's funeral, my father in-law came to me and said, "Kip, I know you have to do what you have to do" code for 'find my grandchildren another mother,' "and we would like to take Victor and Kathy off your hands. When you're ready, you can have them back." Lester and Maxine Bennett were wonderful people, and I knew my children would be in good hands until I could find us a new mommy.

I was sharing an apartment with Denny Christiansen, my beauty supply salesman. He was a man who marked the label of his milk with a razor blade to make sure I wasn't drinking any of it. One evening, I was seated on the couch in our living room, when Denny came over with a shotgun, pointed it right into my face, and said, "You've been drinking my milk!" I grabbed the barrel of the gun, twisting it at the same time, and disarmed him in a flash. If you're going to point a gun at someone, don't get within arm's length of them.

I stood up, walked out the door, down the stairs, and threw the shotgun as hard as I could into the middle of an adjacent cornfield. When I got back to our apartment, he asked me what I had done with his shotgun. I answered, "I traded it to a milkman for four quarts that will arrive in the morning," and went to my room to go to sleep. There was a new alpha male at the Addotta-Christiansen residence.

I'm not always so nonchalant about weapons. One night I was driving back to our apartment after a long date. As I drove, I undid my belt, unbuttoned my pants, unzipped my fly, and let my belly relax. As I turned onto the road that led to our building, there was a roadblock and a police officer in the middle of the road waving me to stop. But from my perspective, it looked like he was waving me ahead, so I gunned it! The officer pulled his weapon and pointed it at my head through the windshield. I slammed on the brakes and came to a halt. Then the officer came over, opened my door, and pulled me out of the car. It seems that there had been a bank robbery in the area, and the cops were skittish about anyone who wasn't heeding their directions.

As I stood there with a service revolver in my face, I noticed that the barrel was shaking. This policeman was even more frightened than I was. To add insult to injury, my trousers fell down around my ankles. There I was, standing in the middle of the road in my own headlights with a cop holding a gun in my face and my trousers down around my ankles.

Of course, he asked me for my ID. I told him it was in my pants. That's when he noticed that my pants had fallen down around my ankles. He said, "Jesus Christ, pull your pants up, man!" I gave the world one of those Oliver Hardy expressions, bent down and pulled my pants up, buttoned them, zipped up my fly, and buckled my belt. Then I reached in my hip pocket, pulled out my wallet, and handed one of Rockford's finest my license. The cop, in turn, took my license and realized he couldn't hold his gun on me and read my license at the same time. So he called his partner over and handed him the gun. I felt like I was in a silent movie. After much studying and conversing, the cop gave me my license back, and his partner handed him his weapon. Then I got in my car and drove the one block to our building.

When I walked into the apartment, Denny Christensen asked, "What have you been doing?"

I said, "Oh nothing," and went to the bathroom to take a pee. When I finished shaking the dew off my lily, I zipped up my fly. How many times does a man have to catch his pecker in his zipper before he learns not to do it again? Evidently seven, because that's what the tally is so far in my life. Roll credits.

A New Wife for Me and Mom for My Kids

One day, a girl named Lynn Johnson came into my beauty salon to have her hair done for her prom. I was immediately interested in her but didn't say anything. As time went on, she came back in to have her hair done many times and we became closer. Slowly I built up the courage to ask her out. When I did she turned me down, saying that she didn't like the car I was driving, a Ford Fairlane. I understood that! In those days girls picked boys with hot cars. So I traded my Fairlane in and got a Dodge Charger. The next time Lynn came into my salon, I took her out to see my new car. She loved it, and this time when I asked her to have a date with me, she said yes. We dated for a little over a year. Actually, we were doing a little more than simply dating.

During that time we made regular visits to Lester Bennett's farm to see my children. I wanted my mother-in-law and father in-law to approve of Lynn and my children to bond with her, and they most certainly did.

One day, in 1967, Lynn called me to say that she was pregnant. I said, "Lynn, I love you. Let's get married."

She said, "You don't have to do that."

"Lynn, I love you," I said again. "You're pregnant with our baby, and I want to do it."

Shortly after that we visited the farm as usual. I took my little boy, Victor, aside and asked him if he thought Lynn would be a good mommy for him. His eyes got big and he said, "Yes, Daddy! I think Lynn would make a good mommy." I asked Victor, who was then six, to go over and ask Lynn if she would marry his dad and be his mommy. He did, and she accepted his proposal.

Lynn and I were married soon thereafter. Lynn, her mother, and I went to the courthouse to see the Justice of the Peace. As soon as the ceremony was over, we drove out to the farm to get my children. No honeymoon! Instantly, Lynn became the mom of two on the day of our marriage. When Lynn gave birth to my son Frank, it was 1968, and Frank was a fine baby!

We spent the next few years poor, but happy. The five of us lived in a modest home with our dog, a Great Dane. Duke was huge and stood forty-three inches at the shoulder. What a wonderful animal. He loved all of us and we him. The best dog I've ever known. As big as he was, he never broke any of the little porcelain or glass pieces we had on the coffee table and end tables. He would come between the coffee table and the couch, realize where he was, and carefully back out.

I miss Duke. When we eventually moved to California, we had to give Duke up to some friends. Later, when we visited them, they had given Duke to a butcher who used Duke as a guard dog at night, keeping him in the basement during the day. I didn't have the courage or heart to visit Duke.

Then, a couple of years later, I decided to rectify this. I went back to Rockford to visit Duke. I was in a large grassy area behind the butcher shop, quite a ways from the building. The butcher let Duke out the back door, and Duke immediately spotted me. He ran to me and was so excited that urine was coming out of him as he ran. I knelt down, and he jumped on top of me, getting pee all over me. I didn't care. I'm sure Duke thought I was there to rescue him, but that was not to be. Duke and I visited for more than an hour, and then I had to leave. I don't have to tell you how I felt. But I swallowed hard and left and was ashamed of myself.

We all must make difficult decisions in life. My obligation was to my wife and children. Everything else took second place. I'm sure my children were and are unaware of my conviction. Maybe someday they will look back and understand that, with few exceptions, my life has had one purpose: to see that my children were safe and sound. My childhood, being what it was, determined my actions.

BUDDY HACKETT

Buddy Hackett was appearing at The Mill Run Theater near Chicago. I heard he was going to do a meet-and-greet in Rockford, Illinois, to kick off a new business called The Globe Glass Company. This was obviously a favor to a friend in the Mob. I arrived early at the location and, sure enough, there was Buddy Hackett getting out of a long black limousine.

He came inside and began to work the room, shaking hands and making small talk with his fans. I waited for some time, gathering the courage to approach him. When I did, I said, "Hello, Mr. Hackett. My name is Kip, and someday I want to be a comedian. I wondered if you could give me some advice."

He said, "Listen, kid, I don't have time right now, but if you come to The Mill Run Theater this Saturday, your name will be at the door. You can come backstage after the show and we'll talk."

I couldn't believe how approachable he was! On Saturday afternoon I drove the eighty miles to The Mill Run Theater. Sure enough, he'd left my name at the door. I took my seat, and, before long, Buddy Hackett came on stage with no introduction. He did an hour and a half, and he was brilliant. The audience was rolling in the aisles and gave him several standing ovations.

After the show I went to the backstage area and told the guard my name. The guard went back and returned to say that Mr. Hackett would see me in a few minutes. Soon, just as promised, I was ushered into Mr. Hackett's dressing room. There was Buddy Hackett, sitting on the couch, wearing the most beautiful, white, terry cloth robe I had ever seen. He looked like a porcelain doll. He sat with me for over an hour and answered every stupid question I asked with patience and grace.

He talked to me about his life. Even though he was the highest-paid entertainer in the world at the time, he said he still didn't know how he had the nerve to go onstage. He meant that he was still learning and that he would never know it all. He was humble and gave me information that would have taken years to learn by myself.

I met Mr. Hackett a few more times over the years, and he was always a wonderful gentleman to me and seemed proud of my success.

Hit 'Em Where They Ain't

William Henry "Wee Willie" Keeler (1872-1923) was a Major League baseball right fielder who played from 1892 to 1910, primarily for the Baltimore Orioles and Brooklyn Superbas in the National League, and the New York Highlanders in the American League. Keeler, one of the best hitters of his time, was inducted into the National Baseball Hall of Fame.

When asked what his philosophy was when hitting a baseball, he said, "Hit 'em where they ain't!" In other words, he would hit the ball to an area where there were no outfielders who could easily catch it.

This has always been my attitude about comedy. Audiences believe they know in advance what the show will be like, simply because there is a comedian appearing. Not in my world! I would not and have not ever done anything that the audience expects me to do. If they think I will arrive on stage, I will appear from the back of the room. If they think I will attempt to be funny, I will begin the show on a sad note. If the audience believes that comedians pick on the audience members, they would be wrong.

I don't want the audience to presume anything about my performance, except that it will be entertaining, and I do have an obligation to attempt to make it so.

I believe that the general public and, I'm sorry to say, most comedians think there is some sort of set choreography that all comedians are bound to follow. Of course, this isn't true. Each and every fine comedian presents their show in a special and different way.

The great Dick Shawn is a perfect example of this. Mr. Shawn always found a way to do things like no other. After seeing him perform one night, before I had begun my comedy quest, I asked him for some advice. "Mr. Shawn, how do you begin a show?" I asked.

He leaned in close and whispered into my left ear, "Don't worry about the first five minutes."

As I look back, this is some of the best advice I've ever gotten. I have never been overly anxious to get that first laugh. I let the audiences' expectations build and watch them lean forward in their seats until they're about to burst with anticipation, and then, and only then, do I give them release from this tension. This, of course, makes that first laugh much bigger than it would have been if I had hurried to get it out.

This technique is one of the tricks of the trade. I will expose the rest of them later on, but first I want you to know more about my background and the experiences that led me to a career in comedy.

GRAMER AND ADAMS

A feeling in my stomach told me I was about to make a life decision. I hired a man at my beauty salon named Bill Gramer. He was a tall, good-looking man who wore a toupee. He wasn't a very good hairdresser, but he had an interesting side.

Bill Gramer was also a musician. He played the trumpet and valve trombone. My ears perked up! Without really discussing this with my wife, Lynn, I began to scheme. I had no experience onstage, so I thought having a band would be a good way for me to break in. I talked to Bill Gramer about it, and he liked the idea. I asked him what role he thought I should play in the band. I didn't play an instrument; as a matter of fact, I even had trouble blowing a whistle! He told me I could play the conga drums and be a singer. So we drove to Chicago to buy that set of drums.

I didn't tell him, but I had already been doing my homework. After we acquired the conga drums, I told him I wanted to make one more stop and gave him the address. We went to see a lady at an agency called Jade Enterprises. Before we entered her office, I told him, "Follow my lead and everything will be fine." The fact is I had no plan and didn't know what in the world I was going to say. I was bluffing!

It was a small office with one desk, and a tall, beautiful, almond-colored woman, Melba Caldwell, was sitting behind it. We introduced ourselves as Gramer and Adams, and I told her we had a band. Bill chimed in and said we had a piano player, a drummer, I played the congas and sang, and he played the trumpet and doubled on valve trombone. She asked us where we were working, and Bill said, "We're not. That's why we're here to see you." I could tell she liked us, and she promised to book Gramer and Adams.

As we left the office and walked back to Bill's Buick Electra, he started to laugh. I asked him what he was laughing at. He said, "We don't have a drummer or a piano player. All we've got is you and I."

I said, "I know. Find us those people, will you?" He laughed again. Well, Bill Gramer came through big-time.

Before long, I met our drummer, Marvin Stolp, a tall, thin, homely man with long red hair and webbed fingers. However, Marvin had the goods! He's an excellent drummer who can play with taste. Loud or soft. That is the true test of a drummer. Anyone can play loud, but can you play soft?

Then Bill introduced me to our piano player, Alfie Braun. And Jade Enterprises did, indeed, start to book us. We were making $900 a week and splitting it four ways. That was a lot of money in 1968, for crying out loud! And eventually we brought it up to $1,200 a week.

The most interesting member of our band was our piano player. Alfie Braun was of average height, with dark hair and a beard. He smelled of a mixture of whiskey and dirty socks. As it turns out, he was the best piano player I've ever known. Alfie Braun's left hand was so powerful that we didn't need a bass player.

The one weak link in the chain was me. I had a problem singing. I was flat. But Alfie Braun always had my back. During each tune he would plink the key note *plink, plink, plink* and keep me on course. When I strayed off course, *plink, plink, plink*, came the key note again.

Alfie Braun also had my back offstage. He had a black belt in karate and, by the way, was a functioning alcoholic. Between sets, Alfie would brood at the bar, drinking his whiskey out of a double glass with ice. If anyone bothered Alfie, he would drink his whiskey down, turn the glass upside down on the bar, and karate chop it in half. If anyone bothered me and they did, he would slip quietly off his barstool, come over, and deck them.

Alfie Braun was a wonderful man, and I'll never forget him. He was the gentlest soul I've ever known. I loved that man.

We traveled the northern Illinois area and played clubs. One night, in a club called The Golden Coin in Gary, Indiana, I had finished singing our first song and said to the audience, "It's great to be in beautiful downtown Gary, Indiana." Suddenly, a shot rang out from the back of the room. I felt the round whiz by my head. As it turned out, the shooter was a drunken local police detective who took offense at my crack about his town. Nothing was done about this incident, so we simply went on with our show. This was the first of three times I would be shot at during one of my shows.

I would eventually sell the band equipment to Bill Gramer and use the money for what came next.

My Decision to Follow My Dream

I never knew Don Carter, but his bowling alley was the site of my decision to change my life. In 1972, I was sitting at the bar of the Don Carter Bowling Alley on East State Street, brooding over a schooner of beer. I was mulling over my life and the direction it was going. At that time I was still working as a stylist at my own beauty salon, Victor's Beauty, named after my son, and wasn't really making enough money to pay the bills. At the end of the month, I was always around twenty-five dollars short of expenses.

When I was a young child, I watched *The Ed Sullivan Show* on TV, and I was enamored by the comedians I saw. I always thought it would be a wonderful thing to do for a living. Working days in the beauty salon and nights in clubs meant I was seldom home and always worn out. I knew it was time to make the move that I had always dreamt of making.

I made my mind up to call my wife and tell her that I thought it was time. I went to the phone booth at Don Carter's and called my wife, Lynn. "Let's have an adventure!" I said when she answered the phone.

She asked, "What do you mean?"

I said, "*The Tonight Show* has just moved from New York to Los Angeles. You know I've always dreamt about becoming a stand-up comedian. I think this is the time."

To my amazement, she said, "Let's do it!"

LYNN AND I BEFORE WE MOVED TO LA

What follows is some of the first material I wrote, satirizing my own childhood. It worked really well and would get an "aw" from the audience.

"They say that most comedians come from sad childhoods. In my case it's true. My parents didn't like me. My mother used to crap in my diapers and blame it on me. When I got a new bike, my father put mousetraps on the crossbar. But I'll never forget the day my dad taught me how to swim. I thought I'd never get out of that sack."

Our Trip to Los Angeles

Lynn and I packed up an old Pontiac station wagon with all the clothing we could carry. With my wife and three children and the $1,200 I made from the sale of our furniture and my band equipment, we set out for California.

We took the southern route, the Christopher Columbus Transcontinental Highway. As we traveled west, we soon encountered more and more desert land. I began to go into foliage shock, for I had never seen a desert before. I was used to the lush forests and the green of Illinois. The further west we got, the more I felt like we were on a different planet. It disturbed me, and I began to feel uneasy.

After three days we reached Needles, California, and checked into a motel. It was night when we arrived, and the next morning we stepped outside to find nothing but sand as far as the eye could see. To me, it looked like the surface of the moon.

It seemed that we would never get to Los Angeles, but after another full day

of driving we arrived in the San Fernando Valley and checked into another motel.

The next morning we began looking for a home, and we found one two bedrooms and one bath for $213 a month. At least we would have a roof over our heads. We had no furniture, so we all slept on the floor, Lynn and I in one bedroom and our three kids in the other.

Things were tough for us. For dinner we would have Hamburger Helper. We would go to secondhand stores and buy sticks of furniture, and we would always keep an eye out for things that other people put out in front of their homes for pick up. Our kids started school, and we began to feel at home in the land of the angels.

MY FIRST PUBLICITY PHOTO

When stand-up comedy hit, it was like a huge rogue wave rising out of the middle of a dead-calm sea. All of a sudden this wave rose up from the depths and was there! It hit the entire country at the same time, like a tsunami coming out of nowhere and hitting an ocean liner, knocking it over onto its massive side.

In the early 1970s, comedy clubs opened across the country. Stand-up comedy was everywhere, and everyone wanted to see it. Even though stand-up comedy had been around for hundreds, if not thousands, of years, everybody rediscovered it.

Comedy clubs in Los Angeles were packed, and the audience often included movie and television stars like Diana Ross, Neil Simon, Roy Rogers, June Allison, and many others. People had been watching Johnny Carson's stand-up comedy for decades on *The Tonight Show*, but for some reason, it had been rediscovered and reborn.

Only by coincidence, I arrived in Los Angeles just before this wave hit. What follows is a story about me, Kip Addotta, a man who rode that comedy rogue wave until its end and beyond.

The next morning I began to look for work and, for some unknown reason, I found myself at NBC Studios in Burbank. Across the street from NBC there was a restaurant called Chadney's. I went in and asked for a job, and they told me that they needed someone to park cars during their lunch hour. This was perfect, because it left me with the rest of the day to follow my aspirations in comedy. I made about fifteen dollars a day.

One day, a pretty young lady approached me and asked if I had ever thought about acting. Her husband was the producer of a soap opera called *Days of Our Lives*. I couldn't believe my ears. I said yes, and she set up an appointment for me to meet her husband the next afternoon after the lunch hour.

I walked across the street to NBC, and my name was at the guard gate. I went in and met with the producer, Ted Corday. I was cast as the piano player at a nightclub called Doug's Place that was featured on *Days of Our Lives*. I did thirteen episodes, and although I really couldn't play the piano, the angle they shot me from made it look like I was playing as I moved my hands back and forth over the keys. It was wonderful and not only provided me with some income, but it also enabled me to get my AFTRA, the American Federation of Television and Radio Artists, union card.

Also, during that time I met a man at Chadney's who struck up a conversation with me. I told him about my plan to be a comedian, and he mentioned that a new nightclub called The Comedy Store had opened up two weeks earlier. That same night I was there and went on stage at 1 a.m. for five long minutes. I was the matter that gathers between your toes after a long run. I was the orifice of Sammy Davis Jr.'s anal canal. My performance stank like dirty armpits. I was as attractive as a semen stain on a bathroom wall. The audience ignored me as if I were a fart in church. I was terrible, but I had broken the ice.

The Comedy Store was the premier comedy club in Hollywood and, indeed, the nation. It was run by Sammy Shore and Rudy De Luca. Rudy was the real writer behind Mel Brooks. He worked for Brooks and wrote all the movies that Brooks was credited with writing. Rudy also wrote all of Sammy Shores' material. Rudy was a genius comedy writer.

In those days, comics were not given specific times to go onstage at The Comedy Store. We would all show up at eight p.m. and wait until Rudy pointed to one of us and said, "You're up."

Sometimes I would approach him and ask, "Rudy, can I go up?"

Rudy would say, "No. You're not a heavyweight!" and walk away. Rudy was a tough taskmaster, but we all loved him. Most times I wouldn't get on until one a.m., but that's the way Rudy rolled.

Sammy Shore was not always there, but when he was, he would go on stage at prime time and take the house down. Much of the time he was on tour with Elvis Presley. Opening for Elvis was a tough spot, because the crowd was there to see Elvis, and only Elvis. Sammy was there to stall until Elvis was ready. The audiences didn't pay any attention to Sammy, and he went many years without getting one laugh.

But Sammy had put his time with Elvis to good use. Sammy didn't know that there was an author traveling with the tour and writing a book entitled, Elvis on Tour. Eventually, Sammy's wife, Mitzi, read the book and found out that Sammy, according to the book, was screwing everything in a skirt. Mitzi immediately filed for divorce. She got the family home and The Comedy Store in the divorce settlement. Sammy got all the other real estate they had purchased together. As it turned out, Mitzi got the better of the deal. She went on to make millions of dollars with The Comedy Store, while Sammy struggled to keep the apartment buildings afloat.

In 1974, when Mitzi Shore took over The Comedy Store, the comedy boon began. The club was successful and packed every night. People from all over the world were coming to witness this new thing called stand-up comedy. The problem was that Mitzi Shore didn't know the first thing about stand-up comedy or running a nightclub. The powerful new wave of comedy was so strong that it would cover up Mitzi's blunderings.

The first thing she did was to begin having affairs with any comic who would have her. And, of course, those comics would get the best spots. The rest of us were left flapping in the wind and had to fight for stage time. If there was a showcase, when network people came in looking for new talent, the rest of us could not get onstage. But the comedy wave was so strong that it didn't matter how many mistakes Mitzi made; people kept coming.

CBS put Mitzi on retainer to look for young acts that would be candidates for TV shows. After eight months, they realized that Mitzi had no clue what she was doing. CBS paid her off, severing their relationship. How embarrassing! The biggest mistake Mitzi made in her dealings was to charge studio executives when they would come to The Comedy Store, and they took it as an insult. The executives stopped coming in altogether. In the end, The Comedy Store did not affect me negatively.

I was writing every waking moment. I watched David Brenner, who I knew from watching TV back in Rockford. I liked his style, and since I had not found a style of my own yet, I used his, not his material, of course, but his style. This worked for me. I did the same with Steve Martin and Albert Brooks. I tried everything I thought of, having heard David Brenner say, "There's something funny about everything."

I didn't have the luxury of cherry-picking the ideas I got, and many times jokes that I had little faith in worked quite well. So take my advice: don't dismiss any idea. You never know when you have gold until you pan it out, as they say.

While the other comedians thought it was enough to do one club a night, I did five! None of the other comedians knew I had a wife and three children, because I never talked about it, but that's what a man with three children does, five clubs. At this point in my career I was doing open mic sets everywhere, every night, seven days a week. I did sets every night at The Comedy Store, Ye Little Club, The Palomino Lounge, The Improv, and a place called Show Biz.

Most comedians today are doing comedy to become famous. I was doing it to become funny enough to make money. Becoming famous never entered my mind. Desperation is a great catalyst. I worked harder than I had ever worked in my life, and I had worked very hard!

Back in Rockford, Illinois, I was broke and had a wife and three children. Now, I was broke, had a wife and three children to support, and I was in Los Angeles with the goal of becoming a comedian. Failure was not an option! I couldn't go back home with my tail between my legs. I was certain that I would be mocked by everyone I knew. "Are you stupid?" they would surely say. "Did you really think you could pull up stakes and move your family to Los Angeles and become a comedian? What were you thinking? What an idiot you are! You're a husband and father, and you put your family in terrible jeopardy to follow a silly dream. Now you have nothing! Who did you think you were, some sort of star? You're nothing and you never will be anything! You're a miserable failure!"

I was driven to make a go of it. With these fears in the back of my head, I spent every waking hour working on material. I also did anything I could to further my goals.

I actually wrote notes on little pieces of paper and stuck them in every phone booth I saw. The note read, "Kip Addotta is a funny man!" And I included my phone number. These notes were in hundreds of phone booths around Hollywood, and I would go back and resupply them regularly. That's how determined I was to make good on my goal. As I've stated, I was driven.

I learned early on that hanging around other comics was a waste of time. What could I learn from them? They were beginners like me and didn't know any more than I did. For the most part, I kept to myself. I found that other beginners loved to talk about comedy and acted like they knew what they were talking about. They did not. And trading ideas with them only gave them the opportunity to steal the ideas that I had come up with. And they did.

When I went around doing sets at night, I watched my so-called friends doing jokes that I had discussed with them only the day before. If I confronted them, they got angry and denied they had gotten these ideas from me.

I liked Steve Martin. He played the banjo, and how could one help but like a guy with a banjo? So I borrowed a banjo from a man and brought it onstage with me. It seemed to work for a few weeks. Then one night, I finished my set, took the banjo, and left the stage. The club owner came up to me and told me never to come back. I asked him why, and he said it was because I didn't play the banjo. So I was fired from a job that I wasn't even getting paid for. I gave the banjo back to the man I had borrowed it from and never used the banjo ploy again.

SCHWAB'S DRUG STORE

For those of you who don't know, George Plimpton was a writer who would do things for the first time and then write about his experience. In 1963, Plimpton attended preseason training with the Detroit Lions of the National Football League as a backup quarterback and ran a few plays in an intrasquad scrimmage. These events were recalled in Plimpton's best-known book, Paper Lion, which was later adapted into a feature film starring Alan Alda, released in 1968.

Plimpton revisited professional football in 1971, this time joining the Baltimore Colts, where he faced his previous team, the Detroit Lions, in an exhibition game. These experiences served as the basis of another football book, *Mad Ducks and Bears*, which dealt primarily with the off-field escapades of football friends such as Alex Karras and Bobby Layne. Another sports book, *Open Net*, saw Plimpton train as an ice hockey goalie with the Boston Bruins, even taking part in a National Hockey League preseason game.

I did this line at The Comedy Store: "I dreamt that I was being prepared for open heart surgery, and out of the corner of my eye I see George Plimpton scrubbing up."

I learned a lesson regarding comedy material. The lesson was, if you do it, they will steal it.

Just as predicted, comedian Jackie Gayle was quoted in *Variety* for using this exact joke the next night at The Playboy Club in Los Angeles.

At Schwab's Drug Store, a hangout for comedians, I confronted Jackie Gayle and told him that he was using my joke. He said, "Don't worry about it, kid. We won't ever be working in the same rooms." He turned out to be right. He worked in the lounges in Las Vegas, and I would end up working in the main rooms!

A persistent Hollywood legend has it that actress Lana Turner was discovered by director Mervyn LeRoy while at the soda counter at Schwab's Drug Store. While the sixteen-year-old Turner was indeed discovered at a soda counter, the actual location was not Schwab's. It was another Sunset Boulevard establishment, the Top Hat Café, and the person who discovered her was not LeRoy, but *Hollywood Reporter* publisher William Wilkerson.

Every day I would go to Schwab's and have a cup of coffee. There I met a writer, Dick Clair, formerly of the comedy team Clair & McMann. When I met him he was the writer and creator of many top television shows. One day he took me to the home of mega movie director George Cukor and introduced me to him.

Dick Clair lived right around the corner from Schwab's. I would visit his apartment and ask him questions. One day I was frustrated about my progress. I told him I wanted to be a comedian and that I was tired of telling people that I was trying to be one. He gave me some very simple advice. He said, "Don't tell them that you want to be a comedian. Tell them that you *are* a comedian."

This simple and rather obvious statement was one of the best pieces of advice I was ever given. Those profound words of wisdom changed my life.

By the way, the great Dick Clair's brain is now cryogenically frozen, like Walt Disney's.

The Real Kramer

I was willing to do anything to get some money coming in, and, as always, the Good Lord provided me with a resource.

He was a tall, dark, thin, handsome man with a big mustache and wild, bushy hair. We hit it off and would travel together from club to club every night. This man was responsible for the beginning of my career. His name was Kenny Kramer.

I met Kenny Kramer on my first visit to The Comedy Store. This was the same man that Michael Richards characterized on *Seinfeld*. Even though he refused the opportunity to meet him, Michael Richards played Kramer to a tee. He was the same man that I began to hang out with in Hollywood. He remains a good friend.

On New Year's Eve of 1973, I was to go on late, as usual. Kramer talked me into taking my clothes off and putting on a makeshift diaper to go onstage at midnight as the Baby New Year.

No sooner had I counted down the New Year when Kramer ran onstage and ripped the diaper off me. To this day, I have the dubious distinction of being the only person to have ever been naked on The Comedy Store stage. Thanks, Kramer.

Kramer has always had a gift for making money. As some of you may remember, during the disco years people wore these little blinking LED lights on them. Those of you who were there will remember those lights blinking everywhere, adding to the excitement of the disco experience. Evidently the people who made the movie *Saturday Night Fever* were not aware of this, the idiots, because they were not used in that movie. Kramer invented those blinking lights. He had them made for thirty cents and sold them around the world for twelve dollars!

Anyhow, one day I told Kramer that if I didn't start making some money soon, I would be in big trouble. He told me that he had been to Miami and there was work there, but we would need some money to make the trip.

Kramer had met a man who had temporarily rented a room in his building. As they were talking, the man told Kramer that he was in Los Angeles for the Super Bowl, which was being played on January 14, 1973, at the Los Angeles Memorial Coliseum. The man told him that he sold souvenirs and that he needed to pick up a couple of guys to help.

At 4:30 on the morning of the game, Kramer and I climbed into a dark blue Ford van with three other guys, and the five of us headed for the LA Coliseum. The van was filled to the rafters with all kinds of cheap, crappy, Miami Dolphins and Minnesota Vikings memorabilia. There were pendants, hats, foam fingers, T-shirts, chalk statues, and everything else you can imagine.

When we arrived at the Coliseum, we were informed that we would not be allowed to actually go inside the structure. Someone else had acquired that contract. We were relegated to working the parking lot. As it would turn out, we got the better end of that deal.

We parked the van and this man loaded us up with all the crap . . . um, memorabilia we could carry. He told us how much to charge for everything, and then he sent us out into the vastness of the parking lot. Personally, I thought this was just another harebrained idea that Kramer had come up with, and we really weren't going to make more than pocket change.

There was no one in the parking lot yet, and it was cold and desolate. I couldn't see any other members of our crew and I was afraid. Then the fans began to arrive! I couldn't believe it. It seemed like there were forty million of them, and as soon as they parked they all came running toward me.

These fans stripped me of everything I had within eight minutes. I had to go back to the van and give the boss all the money before he would load me back up with more junk . . . um, memorabilia. As I struggled away from the van, loaded down, the fans came at me again! Again, they stripped me of everything I had within minutes. I think that if I'd wanted to, I could have sold them my now-soiled shorts. Back to the van I went.

This went on all day and into the early evening. By the time the game was over and all the fans had left, my share alone was $850. This was more money than I had ever seen in one day. I took Lynn out for a beautiful dinner that night. With my wife's permission, Kramer and I started to plan for our trip to Miami. I felt like a man!

At 3:30 a.m. I was sleeping while Kramer was driving his Chevy Nova. We were on the Kentucky Bluegrass Turnpike, when I was rudely awakened by the sound of a siren. I opened my eyes, and we were lit up like a Christmas tree.

The police officer had pulled over two long-haired hippy-types for speeding. He asked, "Do you boys know how fast you were going?"

We said, "No."

The officer asked us to get out of our car, led us back to his cruiser, and pointed at his radar. He showed us that we were doing ninety miles an hour in a fifty-five-mile-per-hour zone. (Due to the Arabian embargo on us, fuel was in short supply, and the government had lowered the speed limit from seventy to fifty-five mph.)

The officer also informed us that we would get a $400 ticket, and since we were from out of state, he would have to impound our car. To top it off, he said we could be doing thirty days in jail.

My mind was spinning. There was no way we could spend thirty days in jail or, in reality, afford a $400 fine. This couldn't happen! My first thought was to kill the officer. I thought better of that, since he was armed and we were not. I'm smart that way. I gathered all the courage I could muster and said, "Officer, couldn't you just cut off all our hair and beat the shit out of us?"

Well, the officer started laughing and said, "What are you guys, a couple of comedians?"

I said, "Yes, officer," and we showed him our pictures and resumes.

Finally he said, "Well I guess I can let you two go, but take it easy."

I don't know where that line came from, but somehow I had pulled it out of my butt and said the right thing at the right time.

We arrived in Miami two days later, having sampled grits along the way. When we arrived in Miami, at Kramer's advisement, we met with a lady named Candy Casino who booked entertainment for cruise ships. She said she would send us to a retirement home, and I could do a free show for the residents.

When I was introduced that evening at the Retirement Home, I heard a sound that I had never heard before. I couldn't figure out what it was, but I would soon find out. The room was full of elderly men and women seated at long, narrow tables, and at each of their place settings was a small wooden mallet. Instead of applauding or laughing, they would beat on their tables with their mallets. When I told this story onstage, I always explained it by saying, "This kept them from laughing so hard they would wet their pants, causing foul stenches and puddles throughout the room."

They must have liked me, because I got a lot of mallet-beating after every joke. Candy Casino, however, didn't think I was suitable for cruise ships. So we didn't find any work, but I did get my first experience working to a Jewish audience.

One day, Kramer and I were driving around, and we came upon a large Victorian home. Although it was dilapidated, we could tell that at one time it was a grand abode. Hanging around in front and on the porch, which encircled the entire structure, were what must have been around forty hippies, both male and female. Well, Kramer couldn't pass this up, so we stopped and introduced ourselves. They all seemed happy to meet us and were especially interested in the fact that we were from Los Angeles. This fact made us instant celebrities. They could not have been more hospitable.

The boys all seemed to want to get us high, and the girls all seemed to want to have sex with us. The leader of this bunch was a short, stocky man with long red hair by the name of Cletus Beagle. Cletus informed us that he was a lawyer. He had been diagnosed with terminal cancer with only a few months left to live. Therefore, he'd acquired a Winnebago motor home and drove from Minnesota to Florida, where he would spend his last days on earth getting high and gathering a following of the people we now stood among. Cletus Beagle further informed us that he was there to max out all of his credit cards and live the high life while he was still among us.

He asked Kramer and me where we were staying, and we told him the truth: we didn't have anywhere to stay. Cletus let us know that there was no more room left in the old house or the motor home, so he would have to rent us a room at a nearby Holiday Inn and he did!

After checking into the Holiday Inn, Kramer and I threw our duffle bags into our two-bed room, and then I had to leave for a meeting with Candy Casino. Again, she told me she didn't have any work for me, because, as she said, "I wouldn't fit in." Candy did get a night's work out of me. I wasn't paid, but I'm sure Candy got cash for my appearance. After the meeting, I went back to the Holiday Inn.

When I arrived, Kramer was standing out in front with this silly grin on his face. When I asked him what was going on, he produced an ounce of pot and offered me a joint. I asked him where he got the pot. He told me that Cletus had given it to him in exchange for a place to sleep that night. It turns out that the hotel was full, and he needed to sleep in our room, because one of the girls back at the house had threatened to kick his ass. Evidently, she was angry because he had allowed us to leave before she had a chance to have sex with us.

I asked Kramer where Cletus was sleeping, and he said, "In your bed."

"In my bed? If you were going to trade him for a bed to sleep in, why didn't you let him have your bed?"

He smiled that "Kramer smile" and said, "It doesn't matter. We're sleeping together tonight in the other bed anyway."

I thought about it for a minute and said, "Let me have a hit of that joint."

We stayed in Miami a couple of days, and then I flew back to LA. I was glad to get out of that city. While walking around there I had a constant fear of being hit on the head by a coconut. I was afraid, because the coconuts were constantly falling from the palm trees to the ground with a thud.

As far as I know, Cletus Beagle is still alive and kicking. You see, I never believed that story about him having cancer. I think he was simply playing the C card to get into girls' pants. Good for you, Cletus!

Not long after that, Kenny Kramer moved back to Manhattan and got an apartment across the hall from Larry David, the co-creator of *Seinfeld*. The rest is history.

After a few months I received a call from an agent, Fred Lawrence. Lawrence had moved to Los Angeles from Miami, where, he said, he'd met Kenny Kramer and loved his material. He said he told Kramer that he needed an act for the next night at the Sahara in Lake Tahoe, opening for The 5th Dimension. Kramer went on to tell this Fred Lawrence guy that if he liked Kramer's style, he was sure to like Kip Addotta's (wink, wink; nudge, nudge).

Fred Lawrence asked if there was anywhere he could see me perform. I told him that he could see me at The Ice House in Pasadena. He and his wife came to my show that night and liked me. The next day I was booked at the Sahara Tahoe! I was opening for The 5th Dimension and making $1,000 for three days. There was a caveat to the contract; if I didn't do well on the first show, I would be flown back to Los Angeles the next day but paid for all three days' work.

That first night, I was backstage, waiting to go on, and I had a tremendous adrenalin rush. I was nervous, to say the least. Then, I heard another sound that I had never heard. It was the timpani drum heralding that the show was about to begin. It scared the hell out of me! The show went well enough for me to finish the entire engagement. My first job in comedy was at one of the best venues in the world. I was on my way!

MY FIRST MANAGER

In the interim, I was still parking cars at Chadney's in Burbank, California. One day, someone told me about this manager that he knew, Martin. I called Martin and told him that I was a young comedian, and he said he wanted to meet me. That very day I went to his office and met with him. He liked me and signed me to a management contract, and a long relationship began.

Only a few weeks after that, Martin was asked to join a large management company, BNB (Bernard, Neufeld and Bash). As part of the deal, he was able to bring his clients along with him. They were located in a tower at the corner of Wilshire Boulevard and Beverly Drive in Beverly Hills. BNB was the management company for Don Adams, Gabe Kaplan, Don Knotts, Lou Rawls, The Captain and Tennille, The Carpenters, Randy Newman, Jim Croce, Neil Sedaka, John Davidson, and many more, even bigger, acts and now Kip Addotta. In brief, BNB was the largest, the most powerful, and the most profitable entertainment management company in the world.

Because of BNB's powerful position, I began to work all over the country. There were no comedy clubs at that time. I worked real nightclubs places that hosted all kinds of entertainment and always had an orchestra. I found out that it was my choice as to whether the band would leave the stage or stay during my performance. I always chose to have them stay. I enjoyed having those men and women behind me, and they seemed to enjoy being there.

Musicians are great lovers of comedy and would laugh along with the audience. At each club, it only took a few nights before the band would actually become part of the show. They would play music if I requested it, and we would do bits together and have all sorts of fun during my performance.

I would ask them to play something in the key of F. And no matter what they played, I would sing "I'm In the Mood for Love." The audience seemed to delight in the cacophony that would result, and the band would laugh uncontrollably. We would come up with all manner of ridiculous things to do with the band. I loved the musicians!

At some point I got a call from a man who said, "I hate to use the phrase *career move*, but I would like to have you do a set at a charity event at the Roxy on Sunset Boulevard. Every name in Hollywood will be there."

I went onstage that night, and he was right; every star in Hollywood was at this event. The problem was that they were all so busy talking with each other that they didn't see or hear anything I said or did. In other words, they didn't know I was there. The next morning, the *LA Times* referred to me as "the anguished Kip Addotta."

I would redeem myself with another appearance at the Roxy, when I did a set before a young group called Aerosmith. I brought the house down! After my set, the guitarist for Aerosmith, Ray Tabano, came up to me and said, "Wow! What's it like to do stand-up comedy?"

I said, "Imagine if you went out there and everyone in the audience had a guitar and an amp and could play it. But you, of course, had to be the best guitarist in the room to hold their attention."

Joe Perry looked at the floor for a few moments, considering what I had said, and then he looked up and said, "Wow!"

I wrote this joke "I try to look as good as possible. That's why I wear contact lenses. These are my fourth pair, and I think I've finally found some I can be comfortable wearing. I had a lot of trouble with contact lenses at first. I couldn't get used to putting something in my eye, especially something as big as a contact lens. Contact lenses are only small when you lose one. Trying to put one in your eye is like trying to put a hubcap in a penny loafer."

In 1974, between my agent and my management company, I started to get really busy. My next gig was a five-week stint at the Pagoda Hotel in Honolulu, Hawaii. I was working with the female impersonator, Jim Bailey. Mr. Bailey's impersonations of Barbra Streisand, Judy Garland, and Phyllis Diller were uncanny. He became these people! For instance, when he was backstage, it wasn't Jim Bailey you were talking to; it was Barbra Streisand. And Barbra was demanding, rude, and spoiled. Many years later, I met the real Phyllis Diller, and, to be honest with you, Jim Bailey was a better Phyllis Diller than the real Phyllis Diller!

I worked with Jim Bailey in Honolulu for five weeks, and time seemed to stand still. I missed my wife and kids. It began to feel like a prison sentence; it felt like it would never end.

I got island fever. I felt claustrophobic. I began to notice everything on the island was shaped like a pineapple. The ash trays, the lamps, the water tower, and even some of the people looked like pineapples! After all, I was 2,558 miles out in the Pacific on a little speck in the ocean. I couldn't wait to get off that island and go home.

Many of the Japanese people who came to the show were under the impression that I was Japanese because of my last name, and they complained to the hotel about it. Although the shows went well, I was depressed. When I finally got back to Los Angeles, I promised myself that I would never go to Hawaii again. I wasn't able to keep that promise.

BACK TO THE ROAD

Historic Cannery Row is Monterey, California's, premiere destination for great hotels, shopping, dining, family fun, and nightlife. My new agent, Fred Lawrence, booked me for a two-week stint at Barbara Kelly's on Cannery Row. During this engagement I was booked on *The Tonight Show* for the first time.

At this point, I had been doing comedy for eighteen months. I flew back to Los Angeles, did the show, and then flew back to Monterey. After that night's shows, I was invited to celebrate my good fortune at Barbara Kelly's home. As I drove up the tree-lined drive to the house, I couldn't help but notice the chimney. It was shaped exactly like a Coke bottle. When I went in, the party was in full tilt, loud music and packed with people to congratulate me on my first Tonight Show appearance. A young man approached me, reached into his pocket, and produced a chunk of cocaine the size of a baseball. I had never seen anything like it. The party went on 'till the wee hours of the morning. Everyone seemed to have a wonderful time.

About two years later, Barbara Kelly was found dead in her home, seemingly the victim of a break-in gone wrong. I later connected the dots and realized that Barbara Kelly and her husband had been big-time cocaine traffickers in that high-end community. Can you say Mob hit?

Soon thereafter, I went on tour with The Association. They were a great bunch of guys who liked me a lot. We would stay up after the shows, smoking marijuana and laughing well into the wee hours of the morning. I would never have the pleasure of working with them again, but I will never forget the good times we had.

When I did get home I was immediately booked at a place called Tulagi's, in Boulder, Colorado. I was working with a funk band called Graham Central Station. The leader of the band was Larry Graham, formerly with Sly and The Family Stone. The band would come in from the back of the showroom, connected to each other hands-to-elbows, mimicking and making the sound of a locomotive. "Choo, Choo,

Choo." This entrance was creative, effective, and well-received by the audience. All week long, I would pass by their dressing room between performances and see Larry Graham sitting on a chair, covered with a blanket, drinking brandy and shivering. He reminded me of Frank Sinatra in the movie *Man with the Golden Arm*, the story of a heroin addict going through withdrawal. I would soon find out that drugs played an integral part in both music and comedy.

THE TONIGHT SHOW

After eighteen months as a comedian, I was booked on *The Tonight Show*. I believed that I was ready, but as I stood there behind that famous curtain, waiting to be introduced, my heart was beating so hard that I thought it was going to explode out of my chest. I was finally introduced and I walked onto the stage. To my left was Doc Severinsen and his band, with Johnny Carson and Ed McMahon to my right. I had so much adrenaline flowing that even if the building had collapsed around me, I would have finished my set.

After my set, one of the producers and my wife, Lynn, came running over to me. Lynn gave me a hug, and the producer, Jim McCalley, asked me if I had any more material like that. I said yes, and my wife and I could not have been more excited. That night I slept for thirteen hours. It was the first full night's sleep I'd had in eighteen months.

"I didn't come from New York. I wasn't a part of any minority, and I hadn't ever had to sleep in my car. Talk about paying dues!"

My agent booked me at the Caribe Hilton in Puerto Rico. I was working with Barbara Eden of *I Dream of Jeannie* fame. I called Kramer, and he came down to meet me there. He flew in from New York for shits and giggles. Kramer was the perfect buddy to be with in Puerto

Rico. He was working the "Legalizing Marijuana" scam; it worked like a charm on the chicks. Kramer was ahead of his time.

One day we were lounging around the hotel pool, and there were these two cute girls on lounges next to us. It was obvious they were "qualifying" us to see if we were worth their time. One of them asked, "Are you staying at the hotel?"

We said yes.

"Which tower?" they asked.

You see, one tower was more expensive than the other. We informed them about our accommodations, and they were not impressed.

It wasn't until Kramer told them that I was working with Barbara Eden that we were cleared for takeoff. Kramer brought the girls to the show that night as my guests, and after the show, we had a few drinks with the ladies. But I was not interested in taking it any further, so I left them both to Kramer and stayed away from our room for a while, leaving Kramer and the girls with plenty of time to do the deed. I asked Kramer later, and he told me he'd had a wonderful time. However, one of the girls had stolen his gold ring. Live by the sword?

I did have a private lunch with Barbara Eden that week. Nothing but good food and chitchat were on the menu, but it was still fun. After all, being in the company of Barbara Eden was good under any circumstances.

Barbara Eden drew big audiences and wasn't really very good live, but neither was I at that time, although the audiences seemed to enjoy us. The women liked me and the men liked her!

Soon after that, I went back to visit my hometown of Rockford, Illinois. Even though my friends had seen me on television, to them the big news was that I had worked with Barbara Eden. They paraded me around their neighborhoods so I could recount the story about her. They wanted their neighbors to know that they knew a guy who had spent time working with Barbara Eden, thereby increasing their cache in the neighborhood. By the time that day was over, I was exhausted, and my friends were all celebrities!

THE MOB

The Addotta name helped me, without my knowing it. Whenever I traveled east of the Mississippi, there would be a driver waiting in the airport baggage area, holding a large card with my name on it. I assumed that the promoter or club owner had sent the driver. They had not. The Mob had sent these men. They would insist on carrying my luggage and would not accept a tip from me. They would deliver me to my hotel, carry my luggage in for me, and escort me and the bellhop up to my room. I thought, *Wow! I must be important.*

When I went to the lobby every night, I would be directed to my waiting car. Inside the car there would be two large men. The man on the passenger side would get out and open the rear door for me. He never looked me in the eye but would always be scanning the perimeter for some reason.

The driver, without saying a word, would take me to the venue, and the man in the passenger seat would get out, scan the perimeter, and open the rear door to let me out. This man would then walk to the stage entrance and open the door for me, escort me to my dressing room and again open the door, clearing the room before allowing me inside. He would then say his first words of the evening: "I'll be right outside the door, Mr. Addotta. If you need anything, let me know."

I was curious as to what was going on but didn't say anything. When the stage manager would knock on my door and say, "Five minutes, Mr. Addotta," I would open the door and, sure enough, there would be this man standing there, right outside. He would offer me his arm and escort me to the wings. I would walk out, do my show, and when it was over he would be waiting to escort me back to my dressing room. Eventually I would be driven back to my hotel by these escorts.

One day I went down to the lobby to have some breakfast, and I noticed one of these men sitting there reading a paper. He would peek over the paper at me and then go back to reading. After a few days of this, I became aware of the fact that not only was there a man in the lobby, but the other man was sitting in a Town Car out in front of the hotel. When I thanked the promoter for this wonderful treatment, he said that he didn't know anything about it.

Everywhere I went, east of the Mississippi, this would happen. Even though I made no announcement of my travel schedule, there were always men waiting for me at the airport and so on. This went on for years. I finally realized what was happening. There is a limousine service and travel agency on the East Coast, and whenever my name would pop up on a passenger manifest, men would be sent to escort and protect me. I will not mention the name of this company, but if you've ever been to Manhattan or flown anywhere, it's quite possible that you used this company for reservations or limo services.

I also learned that these people owned or were partners in all of the theaters and nightclubs that I was working. The Addotta name was highly respected in these circles because of my grandmother and my Uncle Victor.

Frank Sinatra

I was working in Las Vegas and I got a call from the hotel's entertainment department asking me to participate a roast of Ahmad Rashād, a football player that I had never heard of. I asked around and found out that he was a pass receiver for St. Louis Cardinals.

I went to the hotel where this roast was being held and went up to the ballroom where the roast was being done, and took my place on the dais along with several people and, to my surprise, Frank Sinatra. The MC for this roast was Howard Cosell and after a few performers spoke Mr. Cosell started to introduce me. "This next man is a young comedian who is a regular on the Tonight Show, but that doesn't mean he's funny because you don't have to be funny on the Tonight Show". (Howard Cosell and Johnny Carson were feuding at the time because Mr. Cosell had started doing a talk show that was competing with Johnny Carson.) Mr. Cosell went on, "But the proof is in the pudding so let's find out if he's funny. Ladies and gentlemen Kip Addotta"!

I went up to the podium and did my little bit and it went better than I had expected. When i was done I returned to my seat and Mr. Cosell said, "Well I was wrong, someone from The Tonight show was funny". Then he introduced Frank Sinatra who came to the podium and said, referring to me, "This kid if funnier than all of you bums"! I was shocked that Mr. Sinatra would pay me such a compliment and the audience agreed with another round of applause! But I think it was because none of them liked Howard Cosell either!

Mr. Cosell was in the elevator with Mr. Sinatra and me on the way down to the lobby and he said the strangest thing to me. He said (trying to bait me), "You don't like Jews, do you, Kip." I said that's not true, but I know I don't like you, and he laughed. Mr. Sinatra said, "Addotta, that's a Sicilian name isn't it? Come over and visit with me anytime, at Caesars."

I did, just that, several times and he was very nice to me. I wouldn't say much, I just sat there and watched him get dressed just like I used watch my father when he was getting ready to go out dancing.

Mr. Sinatra was a classy guy and would wear a sort of T-Top underwear that would cover the entire trunk of his body with snaps in the middle of his crotch so that the outline of his genitals wouldn't show through his trousers. His valet George would assist him in dressing

The only time I spoke was when he would ask me a question. He would ask me about women and if I had a girlfriend.

This is one of my favorite memories of my early career! Recently I met his daughter Tina and told her this story!

HECKLERS

Contrary to popular belief, men do not heckle. Women are the hecklers. The reason men don't heckle is that they know there is a good chance they can be punched in the nose at any time, so they are generally quiet during a show. Women, on the other hand, have no fear of being punched in the nose. And after a few drinks, they are very capable of shouting out something disruptive.

Movie directors do not seem to know this fact about hecklers. I have never seen a movie that shows a woman heckling a comedian onstage. In addition to that, I have never seen a movie that showed a comedian doing well onstage. Somehow, directors believe that a comedian is more interesting if they are bombing.

"When it comes to talking there is no way a man can compete with a female simply because of experience. On average a man speaks about two thousand words a day. On the other hand women speak more than twenty thousand word a day. So gentleman be careful. She will say 'Let's talk. I want to know how you feel, I want to know what you think.' Gentleman there is no way you want to get into this conversation and this would be a good time to let a five-foot fart and clear her from of the room!

"She might say, 'I don't know why I'm gaining weight!' You could say, 'Maybe you eat too much.' Should you say it? Noooo! She might say 'I have big bones!' You could say 'Looks like a big ass to me.' Should you say it? Noooo! If she wrecks your favorite car, for no good reason, say she wraps it around some municipal structure, walk up to her and muster all of the sincerity you can and say, 'Are you okay?'"

BACK TO WORK

When I got back to Los Angeles, I went straight to The Comedy Store. I was frantically writing new material and trying it out every night. From The Comedy Store I would go to Ye Little Club in Beverly Hills, a comedy club called Showbiz owned by Murray Langston, later known as The Unknown Comic, and then on to The Palomino Lounge out in the San Fernando Valley.

Every day I spent my time sitting on our living room floor, at our coffee table, writing on a legal pad. I used a lead pencil because I could erase it and easily make changes. I did have some remorse about not having time to spend with my wife and kids, but I didn't have the time. Again, I was demonic.

Every night of the week I made my rounds, working at least five clubs a night, recording every set. The next day, I listened to my tapes, making changes as I went. I would try out each joke three times. If it didn't work, I put it aside and revisited it three months later. If a joke worked, I would stop doing it for fear that someone would steal it and, believe me, they did.

"I've stayed in too many hotels. To me, hotel rooms are all the same. As a matter of fact, I think they're all the same room. I think they move that room around the country with me. You get suspicious when you check into a hotel room and find your own toenail on the floor. And filthy! I stayed at a hotel in Florida that had the biggest cockroaches I've ever seen. Huge! Now, I've slept in a room with roaches before, but I've never had one hop in bed, throw one leg over me, and then whisper, 'Hey, we've got ants.' That's a big cockroach."

That bit was the catalyst for me to write the song "Big Cock Roach." I posed the children and my wife so that they appeared forlorn and pitiful and sent it to every agent there. I wanted them to know that I was serious about working and had responsibilities and family to support. It worked!

The following is the review I garnered for the performances at The Diplomat Hotel in Miami:

"Addotta is definitely not your go out there and waste 45 minutes and they'll think they saw a whole show comedian. He's a brilliant young talent who fuses the memories of the 50s with modern-day life in 'El Lay' to paint a fast paced and delightfully humorous collage.

"P.S. All the sweet young things in the audience fell in love with him. When coupled with his talent, it's a sure thing this kid is headed for more than just another opening act slot."

The Florida Entertainment Writers Association presented me with the Comedian of the Year award for my performances at The Diplomat Hotel in Miami. It was a great honor to win this award, and the vote of confidence made a wonderful upgrade to my self-esteem.

During this engagement, I was introduced to one of the audience members, Griselda Blanco, who was known by many nicknames: La Madrina, the Black Widow, the Cocaine Godmother, and the Queen of Narco-Trafficking. She was an important member of the Medellín Cartel and a pioneer in the Miami-based cocaine trade during the 70s and early 2000s.

I also met Sammy Davis Jr. He was a sweet man. He was working in the convention center at The Diplomat with Liza Minnelli, while Lou Rawls and I were in the main room. I later had an experience with Sammy that I will never forget.

FYI . . . Unbeknownst to me, I had been encouraged by management to sign with and pay $3,000 per month to a public relations firm. Lou Rawls was a vested partner in this company. I was treated like a redheaded step-child, and the only thing they did for me was cash my checks. Beware!

I was once booked at Harrah's in Reno, Nevada, to work with Merle Haggard. How surprised was I when I got there? Merle Haggard wouldn't be performing that night. Something about him being so drunk that he ran his car into a ditch.

The night before, Sammy Davis Jr. had ended his stint at Harrah's in Lake Tahoe. So, Harrah's asked him and his supporting act, Johnny Brown, to come down and fill in for Haggard that night. So, with a night off, I went to the show.

I sat in the back of the room and scanned the silhouettes of an audience that was there to see Merle Haggard. The room was packed.

This crowd was in a rowdy mood, and because there was no room for the waiters to move, they simply brought cases of beer to the perimeter of the audience, and the audience members passed the cases over their heads to their final destination.

I had a feeling of foreboding, but I hoped for the best. Then, it came. The house announcer said, "Good evening, ladies and gentlemen. We regret to announce that Merle Haggard will not perform this evening due to circumstances beyond our control. Now, please welcome Sammy Davis Jr." The crowd murmured and growled in disappointment.

Sammy came out to dead silence. He smiled, palmed the audience, and sang, "I Wanna Do Great Things." When the song ended, there wasn't a sound. Of course Sammy knew he was in trouble but, being a professional showman, he continued. He sang, danced, he did impressions all to no avail.

I was witnessing naked racism. I had never seen anything like it before, and I will never forget it. I never mentioned it to Sammy. However, it made me admire him all the more for working through it.

Years later, I would draw on this experience in Detroit, Michigan. I was booked to work for the city of Detroit. The show was in Shane Park, a public park downtown at Eight Mile Road. I did a show every night to no one. All week there was not one person in the audience, but I remembered Sammy Davis Jr. and did the shows anyway.

I learned more about performing that week than I have ever learned at any time in my career. I had fun with it. I would do a joke and then step down into the seats and laugh heartily at my own joke. I would have standing ovations and do countless encores for my imaginary audience. I had a ball, and I would use this experience for the rest of my life. I made lemonade.

OTHER PEOPLE I HAVE WORKED WITH

Mr. Lou Rawls was a righteous dude, always taking very good care of the musicians and me. After a week at Buddies Place, famed drummer Buddy Rich's club in Manhattan, the club manager came to Lou and told Mr. Rawls that he couldn't afford to pay him. Lou told the manager that he should pay the musicians and me, and he would take it in the shorts. We moved on.

Singer Neil Sedaka had come out with his *Sedaka's Back* album, and I was set to go on tour with him. Our first gig was at the Troubadour in West Hollywood, California. We opened on Thanksgiving night, and I was nervous about my show. Being that it was in town, I knew that my agents and managers would be there. I went onstage that night and did a workman-like job, and Neil Sedaka was great. He sang all of his new cuts and all of his past hits too. This was going to be a wonderful tour!

After the show, I went to Sedaka's dressing room to congratulate him. I found John Byner sitting there, and I could tell that he was not impressed with me. Faint praise and all that. John was making smart cracks about me, and this was a taste of future mocking that I would get from him. John Byner seemed to me to be a bit jealous of the new kid in town. This bothered me more than it should have, because I was a big fan of John Byner. Mr. Sedaka was always nice to me.

I try to be as nice as possible to people. I try to be polite. I try to be kind. Because I've been hit in the face with a pool cue. I can tell you how to spot a man who's never been hit in the face with a pool cue. They're pushy, aggressive, and rude. You show me a man who's been whacked across the nose with the thin end of a pool cue, and I'll show you a polite guy, a man who knows what can happen.

Stanley Ralph Ross (1935-2000) also approached me Thanksgiving night at the Troubadour. Raised in Brooklyn, New York, Ross was now starting his career in advertising with Chudacoff and Margulis Advertising in West Los Angeles, California. Soon thereafter, he went to work as a writer and actor on various television shows. Most notable of the shows he wrote for were cult classics such as the 1960s *Batman* series starring Adam West, and also *The Monkeys*. Ross was sometimes credited as Sue Donem, a pun on *pseudonym*, a perfect example of his sense of humor. Stanley Ross was complimentary about my show, and I was pleased with the encouragement. We would have a long relationship.

Tommy Smothers, on the other hand, is a feisty man who always seemed to be looking for a fight. His brother, Dicky, was friendlier, and we would spend good times together. On one occasion, we spent three days together having fun. Meanwhile, Neil Sedaka and I toured the entire country together, making stops at The Cellar Door in Washington, DC, Philadelphia, Boise, Idaho, and many other cities.

In 1975, I had a run-in with Tommy Smothers in Reno, Nevada, where I met his new wife, Rochelle. She was a lovely lady and the mother of nine children when Tommy married her. She knocked on my dressing room door one night and introduced herself to me as Mrs. Tommy Smothers. She seemed to like me a lot, and we spent many lunches together, though nothing ever happened between us. She was faithful to Tommy, and I was faithful to my wife. Tommy didn't like this at all, but Rochelle and I knew there was nothing to it and continued to lunch together in the hotel coffee shop. I lost track of Rochelle, and when I looked Tommy up on Wikipedia there was no mention of her in his Personal Life section. I hope she is doing well.

My Kids

My son Victor was fifteen and was experimenting with all sorts of things. I had the garage fixed up so that Victor would have his own space. It was cool, with a sleeping loft and built-in desk. He loved it.

Around that time we bought a dog, an English sheep dog, and we named him Watson. My wife had given me a book for Christmas, *The Complete Annotated Works of Arthur Conan Doyle*, so I'd immersed myself in Sherlock Holmes. Hence Watson's name. Watson and Victor were inseparable.

When Watson came down with an illness and died, Victor was devastated. We all were. I'll never forget the sight of Victor crying as he carried Watson's limp body into the house from the garage. It was as if he was hoping I could do something to reverse this calamity. My heart was broken for Victor.

My daughter, Kathy, named after my long-lost sister, is indomitable. Her determination shows in everything she does. She was also a little hellion. She and Victor persecuted my youngest son, Frank, at every opportunity. I felt sorry for Frank, but I was away so much that I couldn't control the situation. Frank was living a nightmare when I was on the road. To make up for this, I tried to give Frank special attention when I was at home. It wasn't easy for Frank. He was a shy guy and didn't readily take to affection. He did join me in my interest in Sherlock Holmes, and we would watch movies together. I wish we could have watched more movies, comparing notes on Sherlock's adventures, but, again, I was gone three weeks out of every month.

One time I came back from the road and Frank told me that I had gotten a call from *Life* magazine. I asked him why he didn't inform his mom, and he shrugged it off with an "I don't know." I didn't scold him for not saying anything. As much as I would have wanted a spread in *Life* magazine, I didn't feel that I should punish Frank. He had enough problems already. I love this kid.

Frank still hasn't found himself, and although he is a good man, I would love for him to excel at something to satisfy his ego. I believe and pray that this will happen. He's certainly bright enough.

Again, when Lynn and I were away, Victor and Kathy would persecute Frank by doing things like using a broomstick to lock Frank in the shower for hours. Frank would just sit there on the shower floor and wait for them to let him out. I didn't find out about this until years later.

Had I known about this at the time, heads would have rolled. Frank tried to follow in my footsteps by experimenting with performance art. He wanted a guitar, and he got one, but nothing ever came of it. This may have been a blessing because his favorite bands were KISS and AC/DC.

Frank is now married to his second wife, Deicy. She is a charming young lady. If I call Frank and say, "Frank, I need your help," he never fails to come to my aid, despite our being estranged.

I know he still loves me, and I am saddened that he is missing out on the good times we could be having now. When I see Frank, I don't say much to him. I want him to see that I have become indifferent to him, and maybe that will snap him out of his present position.

The Memphis Hilton

I've worked Memphis, Tennessee, many times and always had wonderful shows. Mostly, I worked at the Memphis Hilton, a nice place with a great showroom. I worked there alone and also with John Davidson and Tina Turner.

Once while I was there I was asked to be a judge at the annual Memphis Barbecue and Chili Cook-Off. I arrived that morning, starving, and the aroma of roasting pigs was everywhere. However, I couldn't get a bite to eat from anyone, because the judging had not yet taken place. All day long I was craving some pork, any pork. Pork was being cooked in every imaginable contraption, from 55-gallon drums that had been converted into BBQ pits, to even a locomotive containing four full-sized pigs turning on spits. Pork to my left, pork to my right, pork in my nostrils, pork on my clothes pork, pork everywhere, and not a bite to eat!

Finally, the judging began. I tasted every kind of pork imaginable. Red chili, green chili, red and green chili. I tasted and I tasted and, finally, I picked the one I thought was the best. And, indeed, the one I picked won the chili portion of the contest. However, by that time I was so full of chili that I didn't have room for any roast pork.

Once I was there working with Tina Turner, a true professional who had come up, with her husband, Ike, from the Chitlin' Circuit, the name given to rough-and-tumble joints where black acts performed to black audiences. They could be dangerous places. So people like Tina Turner, Redd Foxx, Jerry Lee Lewis, and many more, including me, learned how to perform, honed our acts, and were taught the most important thing about Chitlin' Circuit clubs, which was how to get the money out of the club owner.

This system that all the acts learned and used was simple. In their contracts it was stipulated that they would be paid in cash before each show, and if the club owner didn't fulfill this stipulation, the show didn't go on. The show always went on! In Chitlin' Circuit clubs everybody carried guns, including me. I always carried a heater when I traveled. It came in handy when I went to get paid. I always knew that the club owner had a gun in his desk, and he always knew that I had a gun on my ankle. This knowledge made both of us very polite to one another, and I always got my money, in cash, with no problems. That's the way it was.

So, this is where Tina Turner's roots were planted, and yes, she always carried a weapon. Every night, the manager of the showroom at the Memphis Hilton would bring Tina Turner a brown paper bag full of cash before the show, and only then did the show begin.

When I worked there in front of Tina Turner, I had especially good shows. Tina, although a great entertainer, was having a little trouble following me. When you support a star, it's not your job to try to outdo them. It's your job to hand them that audience on a silver platter. And I wasn't trying to outdo Tina, but no matter how I tried to control the audience, to bring them up to a point of reasonable appreciation, they seemed to go crazy for me.

This did not go unnoticed by Tina. One night before the show, Tina Turner sent for me. I went to her dressing room, where she was putting her makeup on at her dressing table. Without looking away from the mirror, she said, "Kip, that's a great outfit you're wearing." That week my stage costume was a black velvet jumpsuit, light grey shirt, and a black velvet bow tie. It was dazzling! She said, "Kip, I'd like to buy that outfit from you. How much do you want for it?"

You see, Tina Turner surmised that the reason I was doing so well with the audience was because I was wearing this costume. And she may have been right. It was, as I have said, dazzling.

I figured out her motive right away. I said, "Miss Turner, my outfit is not for sale. However, I have a black suit I could wear instead."

Tina Turner said, "That would be nice. Thank you." And she continued doing her makeup without ever looking at me.

The rest of my shows that week were great but not as stupendous as the first few. Tina Turner was right. She was such a pro that she solved the problem and saved my job for me at the same time.

The Memphis Hilton seemed to be a magical place. Many interesting things happened to me there. One night I was standing in the lobby after my show, and a cute little lady wearing a pink Chanel suit and a pillbox hat walked over to me. She said, "Enjoyed your show." With her lovely southern accent, she went on. "My name is so-and-so, and I'm married to a doctor in Boonville, Kentucky. That's Daniel Boone's hometown. And I would love to suck your Yankee dick."

I, with the most gentlemanly manner I could muster, told her that I was flattered but had a previous engagement and was unable to grant her request. Then I made a hasty retreat. I guess this was an example of southern hospitality.

The next night, again, I was standing in the lobby of the Memphis Hilton after my show. There was a tap on my shoulder, and I turned around to see Jerry Lee Lewis standing there. My heart jumped into my throat, and I was unable to speak. He said, "I'm Jerry Lee Lewis, and I enjoyed your show."

I said, "W-w-well, thank you, Mr. Lewis."

He suggested we head to the bar for a drink. I followed him into the bar, and we sat down at a two-top. He was quiet and so was I. We just sat there, sipping our drinks. I think he was drunk.

After about fifteen minutes he said, "Let's take a ride." I followed him out to the front of the hotel, and we got into his Lincoln and took off. I didn't know where we were going, but I remember thinking, *Well, I'm sure this is not the first time he's been drunk and driving, and he is Jerry Lee Lewis . . .* so I figured I would be all right.

Jerry pulled out an open bottle of champagne and was swigging from it as he drove. There was a chrome-plated, pearl-handled, 1911 Browning semiautomatic gun on the dashboard. I didn't say a word. We drove and drove until finally we ended up at Graceland, the home of Elvis Presley.

Jerry Lee pulled up to the gate and ran into it with a thump. He must have thought that his window was down, because he attempted to throw the bottle out. But the window was not down and it shattered, bouncing the champagne bottle back and down into his lap. He didn't seem to notice this. He grabbed the handgun, stuck it through the broken window, and fired three shots into the air. "I'm The King, you son of a bitch!" he shouted. I was beginning to think there was, indeed, going to be trouble.

A few minutes later, two sheriffs' cars pulled up behind us. The larger of the two officers came over to Jerry Lee's window and said, "Now, Jerry Lee, you have to stop doing this. These people need to get their sleep." Then he instructed the other officer to take me home and said that he would see to Jerry Lee. I never heard another word about it.

There was no trouble. Just another night for Jerry Lee Lewis! Years later I would, indeed, meet Elvis Presley under less dramatic circumstances.

In late 1974 I was working the Circus Maximus at Caesar's Palace in Las Vegas, and Elvis had opened a stint at the International Hotel. I knew that, as always, Elvis would have a press party after his opening show, so I called over and asked the maître d' if he would leave my name backstage. He said, "No problem."

The International Hotel, now the Hilton, had the largest showroom in Las Vegas, seating 1,250 people. Elvis was being paid $50,000 a week. Colonel Parker, his manager, took fifty percent off the top, and Elvis got whatever was left after expenses. So if the truth be known, Elvis was losing money on the deal. But it wasn't about the money. He had come out of retirement in 1969 because he missed performing.

I arrived at the International, went backstage, and waited in the press room, which was packed with reporters. By this time, these people had gotten younger and weren't quite as impressed with Mr. Presley as they should have been, but he was still The King, and to further their own agenda they would definitely cover anything he did.

I didn't talk to anyone but simply stood in a corner and took in the scene. Then, after about fifteen minutes, Elvis Presley appeared. To be honest, I couldn't believe my eyes or the fact that I was standing in the same room as Elvis Presley! I watched The King go from person to person and introduce himself to each one. He was most polite and gracious and couldn't have been more cordial. He was a pro. Finally, after some time, he got to me and said, "Hello, I'm Elvis Presley."

I said, "Hello, Mr. Presley, I'm Kip Addotta, and I'm working at Caesar's Palace, in the Circus Maximus."

He seemed to know my name. I chalked this up to him being polite. And he said, "How was your audience tonight?"

I said, "Timid."

"Yeah, ours too," he said. I will never forget this moment of intimacy between me and The King.

A few days later I was pacing around my room and thinking about this little exchange I'd had with Elvis Presley. I threw caution to the wind, called his hotel, and asked to be connected to Mr. Presley's room. To my amazement the call went though and someone answered the phone. I assumed that he was screening his calls through his boys, known as The Memphis Mafia.

The voice on the other end of the line answered with, "Mr. Presley's suite."

I said, "My name is Kip, and I'd like to talk to Mr. Presley."

The voice said, "Kip who?"

In the background I heard Elvis say, "I'll take that call." Then he got on the line. "Hi, Kip."

I said, "Mr. Presley, I've got nothing to do today. Let's go have some fun."

"What do you mean?" Elvis said.

That was a good question, because I had no idea what I meant. Once again I pulled something out of my butt and said, "Let's go go-carting."

The King chuckled and said, "Kip, I can't do that. I'd get mobbed."

"Mr. Presley, take the chrome suit off, put on some jeans and a ball cap, and let's go go-carting," I said. There was a long pause, and somehow I knew he was looking down at his own clothing and realizing he was actually wearing a chrome suit.

He said, "Pick me up out back in thirty minutes."

I got in my car and drove over to the International's stage door. After a time, the door opened and out jumped Elvis Presley. He came over to my car, opened the passenger door, hopped in, and we were off.

"Hi, Mr. Presley," I said.

He said, "You can call me Elvis."

I said, "Forgive me, but I don't think I can!" He chuckled.

We drove to the go-cart track without speaking, rented a couple of carts, and started racing around the track. I wasn't really sure what to do. I had gotten myself into this delightful dilemma and had no idea what I was going to do with it. Then it happened. As Elvis passed me on the right, he swerved to the left, rammed me, and chuckled. We went another lap, and he did it again. I got it. Mr. Presley wanted to play. We did another lap, and as we got to the same place, he swerved again. This time I slammed on the brakes and rammed him. We spent the rest of the afternoon racing around the track like idiots, with no concern for the go-carts. After we had worn ourselves out with laughter and competition, we called it quits and drove back to the International, laughing all the way.

When we reached the stage door, Elvis jumped out of the car and hurried away. Before slipping inside, he looked back at me and said, "Call me tomorrow, Kip."

I smiled. "Okay, Elvis. Thanks."

For that moment in time, in that space in the universe, Elvis Presley and Kip Addotta were buddies. These little excursions happened three or four times during the week, and for those short times he didn't have to be The King, and I didn't have to be a pip-squeak. We never met or spoke again after that week, but I have the satisfaction of looking back on this as one of the greatest pleasures of my life.

On August 16, 1977, I was on my sailboat at Marina Del Rey, pacing back and forth, waiting for an idea to fall on me from Heaven, as I believe all ideas do. The radio was playing in the background when the programing was interrupted by an announcement of Elvis Presley's death. To this day I have difficulty dealing with this loss. And when I think of him, I think of him laughing and poking me and crashing into me on a go-cart track in Las Vegas. What a great guy.

When he was not in school, my son Frank would go on the road with me. Frank won over everyone we met, and he also made it a point to take advantage of the services available in the luxurious hotels in Vegas. One time when we checked out, I noticed a room service charge for chips and dip. Frank had ordered them and had them brought to the room. My wife and I both thought this was very amusing and recounted this story to our friends many times.

Frank was a big KISS fan. Gene Simmons was in the showroom to see Diana Ross perform on a night Frank and I were in Vegas. As you may know, all the members of KISS wore makeup when they performed. I took Frank by the hand and led him to the backstage area, just behind the curtain. We parted the curtain just a bit, and I asked Frank to tell me where Gene Simmons was sitting. He peeked through the curtains and, without hesitation, said, "There he is, in the first booth to the right."

After the show, I went to Gene Simmons and informed him that my son was a great fan and asked if he would stop by my dressing room and meet him. A few moments later, there was a knock on my dressing room door. I asked Frank if he would answer it. When he did, there was Gene Simmons, balancing a long-stem rose on one finger. He came in and took several turns around the room, finally stopping in front of

Frank, and handed off the rose to my son. Gene Simmons has been my hero ever since.

I still see him now and then and always walk over and reintroduce myself. Gene Simmons is not only very bright; he is also a great guy.

My Comedy Material

My comedy material had begun to evolve, and I was becoming my own man. I also began to understand how to deal with an audience. How to mount a stage and where to work on the stage. All of these things meant as much as the jokes, and I began to have strong shows wherever I worked, no matter the size of the audience. Whether I was working to two hundred people or fifteen thousand people, it worked.

Performance is a complicated discipline. Many people, although they're watching it happen before their very eyes, don't see what is really going on. Stand-up comedy is much the same as music. It has rhythm, dynamics, and even melody. Many musicians go on to be comedians. Charley Callis, Henny Youngman, Jack Benny, Steve Martin, Johnny Carson, Woody Allen, and even I, Kip Addotta, all had a musical background.

This musical background gives comedians a head start: timing. One must take music into account to write and perform comedy. People have complimented me on my timing. I get my timing from listening to the audience. Comedy is not about your mouth; it is about your ears. One must listen to the audience and find their rhythm. They will let you know when to resume after a line. It's much like the way an orchestra listens to the drummer to find its timing.

Many beginners are so anxious to get the words out that they ruin their own sets by not letting the audience have a moment to digest the material, much like a young man suffers from premature ejaculation. The audience creates the timing if you're only willing to listen for it.

When I mount a stage, I am not in a hurry to get that first line out. I listen to the audience and let them settle in on me before I begin to speak. During these few moments, I cast my eyes around the audience, looking and acknowledging everyone and no one at the same time. Then, when they're set, I begin. I'll do the first line and let it lay there, listening for the audience to let me know when to continue.

This thing called stand-up comedy looks easy when done by someone who knows what they're doing, but make no mistake: it is not. One must study and put in a lot of time to learn this purest of art forms. They say that to learn anything, it takes ten thousand hours of practice. Well, I've had fifty thousand hours of practice and feel qualified to speak on this topic.

It was 1975, and at that time in my life, I was doing a lot of TV. On many occasions, this required me to be in two places at one time. I would be in Cleveland and get a call from my management company, informing me that I was doing *The Tonight Show* that very evening and yes, they really would call at the last minute. I would use the three-hour time difference in my favor. I'd rent a private jet, fly to Burbank, do *The Tonight Show* which taped at 5:30 in the afternoon get back on the jet, and be back in Cleveland in time to do my ten p.m. show!

One of the jokes I wrote was in reference to the movie Jaws. I would ask, "Why is it that every time they catch a shark and cut it open they always find a license plate in its stomach? Who are these people who drive into the ocean and park near a shark?"

These lines were the impetus for the song "Wet Dream," a narration using calculated malapropisms related to fish, with a Raymond Chandler-style delivery set to original music arranged and orchestrated by Rick Johnston. It took me six months to write and arrange this song, using seafood restaurant menus so that every fish used in the song was recognizable to the listeners. This Raymond Chandler-style delivery prompted me to wear a fedora to fit the role. The song was so popular that one day I got a call from Mason Williams of "Classical Gas" fame, requesting permission for the Seattle Philharmonic to use it in their performances. Of course I said yes and am extremely proud of this tribute.

"Since then he has written many more songs, one another pun-filled ditty called 'Life In the Slaw Lane,' which charted in the top ten and was all about vegetables and landed him a featured article in *People* magazine. 'I stopped writing the pun songs after that, because I had become bored with the style and didn't want to be defined by it.' Other of Addotta's work, to name a few, are 'Big Cock Roach,' 'I Saw Daddy Kissing Santa Claus,' 'I'm So Miserable Without You, It's Just Like Having You Around' (a lament about his upcoming divorce)."

With regular appearances on *The Merv Griffin Show, The Tonight Show, The Mike Douglas Show* (broadcast out of Philadelphia), *Don Kershner's Rock Concert, and The Midnight Special,* I was gone from my family for four weeks out of five. Stress cracks began to show in my marriage. My kids were growing up, and I wasn't there to father them. So, when they were available I began to take them, in turn, on the road with me. I wanted them to see what Daddy was doing when he was gone.

On one of these trips, my son Victor was with me in Lake Tahoe. We went skiing, and I knew that if I was injured I wouldn't be able to support my family, so I stuck to the beginner runs. Victor, fearless to a fault, went on the most dangerous run, The Widow Maker. He set the bindings on his skis too tight and took a fall, breaking his left leg. As a convenience, there was a hospital at the bottom of this run, and he practically tumbled right into the emergency room. The doctors set his leg, and I brought him home to his mom in bad shape.

Fear is always there; it has become my constant companion. If one lets fear rule, one will never accomplish anything in life. You will go to your grave anonymous. And if you're lucky enough to be given life and haven't done anything with it? In my religion, that's a mortal sin. Punishment in the afterlife will be yours!

PHOTO TAKEN TO SEND TO MY AGENTS

In 1977, I was making more money than I could have ever imagined. I wanted to have something our family could do together to bond. So I bought a boat. My wife, Lynn, didn't really enjoy sailing, but she went along with it.

When we weren't sailing, I would spend hours sitting on the boat writing. It helped me concentrate. It was a place where I could be away from our house and the chaos of children running around doing what children do. I seldom talked about my children onstage. I didn't want them exposed to the public and put in jeopardy.

One day on the boat, a joke came to me. It was the years of the Carter administration. President Carter's brother Billy was considered by everyone to be a dolt. So I wrote, "It's not easy to gain the public's trust when you have a brother who's constantly embarrassing you, but Billy puts up with it."

The audiences loved this joke. On *The Tonight Show*, it brought down the house and got a huge round of applause.

As well as the joke worked, it didn't last long, which is the problem with current event jokes. So I never did a current event joke again. I wanted my material to last forever, and it has. That's why comics all over the world have stolen it. It's a fact that bothers me, because it takes forever to write a joke and work it out properly. And here come these idiots who simply put it in their act. Damn it!

That's one of the reasons I don't use opening acts when I perform. They usually demoralize the audience, and when they leave they take my material with them.

When I do see a comic using my material, I call them on it. They look at the floor and say, "I didn't know it was your joke." If you didn't know it was my joke, whose joke did you think it was? If you didn't write it, where do you think it came from? Jokes don't write themselves. These people aren't fooling anyone. People know they've heard the joke before and know they heard it from Kip Addotta.

One time, I heard a comic do one of my jokes and I called out, "That's Kip Addotta's joke."

After his set, this young punk came running up to me in a rage. "Don't you ever interrupt my show again," he said.

I said, "Stop using my jokes and I won't."

He said, "How do you know it's your joke?"

"I know it's my joke, and I can tell you what album it was from, and the album was recorded before you ever started working in the business. That's the proof you're looking for. Now, if you're interested, we can step outside and continue this conversation with our fists, if you'd like."

That always took the starch out of them, and they never had the courage or the gall to do it again. You have to be ready and willing to throw down. If there is no jeopardy, these people have no respect. Someone once said, "I don't care if they like me as long as they fear me."

Don Novello (Father Guido Sarducci) walked into Dan Tana's restaurant one evening with a date, and I approached him. "Hi, Don. Why did you say such insulting things about me on *Second City TV*? My children watched that show." He insisted that he hadn't said anything about me.

Richard Romanus, a cast member on *Second City*, would be introduced as me and would come out and do his bad impression of me and then they would give him the hook. This would happen regularly on the show.

I told Don Novello, "You were the producer of the show and are responsible for its content." He and his lady left the restaurant. These people do not want to be accountable for their deeds.

WOMEN

I've always said that if it were not for women, there would be no such thing as show business. The first dilemma a man has when asking a girl out on a date is, *What am I going to do with her? Where am I going to take her?* Naturally, it will have to be somewhere that will impress her, and what better way to impress her than to take her to a show. The more important the show is, the better. The lady will brag to her girlfriends that the man is taking her out, and the girlfriends will try to qualify the date by how valuable they perceive it to be. Taking a girl to see a band is one thing, but taking her to see the Rolling Stones is a something else entirely.

Ladies perceived me as the alpha male. They liked me because I was the center of attention. This could cause jealousy among the men in the audience, and when you add liquor and weapons and cocaine to the equation, it can become dangerous for the performer. It seemed that almost everyone, including women, was packing heat.

This all came together one night in Atlanta, Georgia. I was onstage, and the ladies were supporting me with great gusto. One of the men took exception to this, pulled out his weapon, and discharged a round in my direction. I saw the muzzle flash and heard the round whiz by my head. Then the couple simply ducked out the back door and disappeared into the night. That was the third time I dodged a bullet. Stand-up comedy can be dangerous!

One night I was working at The Punch Line in Atlanta and from out of the darkness came a large salt shaker that hit me on the head and left a large welt.. Some white man had gotten behind a table of black people and threw it at me trying to make it seem like one of the blacks had done it Then he ran out of the club!

The next day this man called the club and told the owner that I was doing racist material. Luckily the club owner was in the room that night and knew better.

I've never been a ladies man nor did I feel that I was good looking. But, now that I look back I realize that I was good looking. Many women threw themselves at me, but it wasn't me that they where interested in, it was my celebrity. I made a few mistakes and have paid the price for them. My wife divorced me and I went through great remorse because of it. I was always sick to my stomach and the only time this nausea diminished was when I was on stage and able to put it out of my mind. I hurt my wife and my kids and will never forgive myself for such stupidity!

My first wife Mary cheated on me and it made me sick to my stomach, so I should have known better! I forgave her for it and soon after she passed away.

ALLEN NECHY

I was standing at the bar after my first show at a nightclub in Atlanta. This was during my bow tie period. I like bow ties and own about twenty-five of them. As I was standing at this bar, a man walked up to me and asked, "Is the bow tie a trademark of yours?"

I said, "I've never thought about it, but I am wearing bow ties."

To paraphrase Humphrey Bogart in the movie *Casablanca*, "This was the beginning of a beautiful friendship." Allen Nechy is an interesting man. He was a "tin man". In other words, he sold home siding, door-to-door. He came out of Cincinnati, Ohio, where he was knocking on doors at the age of sixteen. We had an immediate affinity for each other. We learned on the street what we knew couldn't be taught in school. Allen learned from wise-guy salesmen.

If someone knocks at your door and he has thick, straight hair that seems to stand straight out from its roots and a space between his two front teeth, don't let him in. Because if you let him in, he's going to sell you something. That's what Allen Nechy did. And don't get into a pool game with him because you will loose your money!

We started hanging out together. Allen was a good guy to hang out with, because he knew everybody in town, at least everybody who was worth knowing. On many occasions I would act up, and someone worth knowing would come over, and Allen would give him the sign that meant, "He's okay; he's with me." We had a lot of fun.

One night Allen and I were out with four or five other men, and we were having a couple of drinks (17 each). We were telling jokes and having the kind of fun that men have. He turned to me with that goofy smile he has and asked, "Have you ever had this much fun with a woman?"

I thought about it for a moment and honestly said, "No, I haven't."

Allen Nechy was a drinker. He would drink a quart of Jack before he went out for the evening. Luckily, he was a happy drinker. But let's back up a little.

Nechy had been in a lot more towns than Cincinnati and Atlanta. He worked all over the Midwest and the South, including Louisiana. In New Orleans he was, as always, a wild child. He loved fast cars and street racing. But the problem with that was that he got a lot of tickets and lost his driver's license. No problem.

Allen went to see the boss of New Orleans, Carlos "The Little Man" Marcello, in his office at the Town and Country Motel, and asked if he could get some driver's licenses with different identities. Mr. Marcello knew Allen. He wrote a little note, signed it, handed it to Allen, and said, "This is gonna be no problem at all, son. Take it down to the DMV. Hand it to the lady behind the counter, and she'll take care of whatever you need. And, by the way, don't be such a stranger, boy."

When Allen arrived at the DMV, he did exactly what Mr. Marcello had told him to do. When he handed the note to the lady behind the counter, she asked, "Well, how many of these do you need?"

Allen said, "I think six will do."

In no time at all he had six driver's licenses with six different identities. Now he could get back to doing what he loved to do, which was street racing, with a valid driver's license. Again, no problem.

I have known this man for thirty-five years. Twenty-five years ago, Allen was in Jerry Seinfeld's hotel room, looped as usual. Jerry said, "Nechy, you have to lose the booze. It's not cute anymore." With that, Allen never had another drink. No twelve-step program. He simply put it down.

Another interesting thing about Nechy is that he never, ever, uses profanity. You can tell if he's disappointed with you when he calls you a goof. And if he does call you a goof, you'd better change your ways.

In 2002, Nechy moved to Los Angeles and applied for a contractor's license. The state of California handed him the test. It weighed six pounds. Allen, a man who can barely read or write, studied the test for six months and passed it. But Allen didn't get a simple contractor's license; he got the biggest, baddest, contractor's license you can get. The kind of license that allowed him to build hospitals, if he wanted to.

With that, he went into business selling home improvements and was doing well. Then the bottom dropped out of the economy in Los Angeles, and before long, he was tapped out. A friend of his invited Allen to stay at his home in Las Vegas. Allen did, but the economy there was lousy too. Allen lost everything he had, his car, everything!

Allen finally found a job in sales. He was the new guy, but within a year and a half he had become the top salesman. Currently he's manager of the entire operation, making great money, driving a Cadillac and back on top of the world. My friend Allen Nechy is no goof!

WATCH YOUR SIX

One night in Cleveland, Ohio, I was having breakfast in a coffee shop after the show. It was 3 a.m. My back was to the door, so I didn't see the man approaching from behind me.

The man reached around, picked up my steak knife, held it to my throat, and said, "Let me hold fifty!"

I thought my life was over! I said, "What the hell do you think you're doing? Are you going to the gas chamber for fifty dollars? Now, put that knife down and get the hell out of here!"

The man dropped my knife and sat down, staring me right in the face. I could tell from his eyes that he was on something. He didn't know where he was. The man got up and ran out of the place and disappeared into the darkness.

Another strange incident happened when my name was on the marquee at Caesars Palace. A guy I will call O'Brien met a girl he liked and to impress her he told her that he was Kip Addotta. He met her parents as Kip Addotta and borrowed three thousand dollars from her father as Kip Addotta and skipped out of town. He avoided them when I was on stage and told them that they couldn't come to the show because it was sold out. Her father called my room and asked me where his money was and I told him I didn't know him. He didn't believe me so I asked him to come to Caesars Palace and he did. I showed him my ID and he left.

And how did I know about this? O'Brien called me and told me about it and how funny it was. What an A Hole

The Spider and the Cricket

"Every man for himself!" It's nature's way. My son Victor found a Tarantula in the forest and brought it home as a pet. We bought a glass tank for the tarantula and would watch it eat. Tarantulas eat live crickets, so we put six crickets in the tank with the spider. These crickets were born and raised in a pet shop. They'd never seen a tarantula before. They didn't know what was going to happen, and they were frolicking around, bumping into the spider's legs. The tarantula was motionless, but as soon as one of the crickets wandered under it . . . *bloop*. It was all over. The tarantula consumed five of the six crickets.

Now, I felt sorry for those five crickets but nowhere near as sorry as I felt for the one cricket that he didn't eat. You see, tarantulas only eat about once a week. So for a whole week, this one little cricket was in that tank, knowing what was going to happen to him eventually.

Before long, this little cricket became a pet to us. We didn't want to see it get hurt. But what were we going to do, play God? Take our cricket out of the tank? After much thought we decided to increase our cricket's odds. We put more crickets in the tank, and you should have seen the look on our little cricket's face when we did that. He was so happy. He looked at the spider as if to say, "I won't say a word," and he told the other crickets, "Come on in, fellows. Just stand over there, under the gazebo."

IN LAS VEGA

Another problem I had was that I had trouble getting sound checks. I solved this with the help of Ronna Wallace, a longtime friend who I had met during my stint in Hawaii. She was always at my gigs; a groupie, if you will. I requested that she go out and rent a nun's outfit. As soon as Diana Ross was done with her sound check, Ronna was to run out onstage in her nun's outfit and politely announce over the sound system that Mr. Addotta would like to do his sound check. You see, sound crews were not used to having a comedian do sound checks and would disappear as soon as the headliner was done. From then on, I always got sound checks.

My personal nun would also assist me in my dressing room. She would answer the door when someone knocked and offer them a cocktail. After our opening in Long Island, there was a knock on my door, and it was a group of five agents from William Morris, headed by Lee Solomon. She invited them in and made them all cocktails. These Jewish men were on their best behavior, and from then on I got anything I asked for. Ronna is a good sport and a wonderful friend. The news that Kip Addotta traveled with a nun spread like wildfire. I was infamous.

Meanwhile my daughter, Kathy, then ten, was traveling with me. Kathy was the most courageous little girl and took to the glamorous life at Caesars Palace without missing a beat. I must say that I was beaming with pride for her, and she was delighted to be with her daddy.

Kathy and I flew home after the Caesar's Palace gig. Then Diana Ross and I flew to New York and opened in Long Island. Diana was staying in her apartment at The Pierre, and I was staying at my friend Kenny Bloom's place.

One day I called Diana and invited her to Resorts International, which had just opened in Atlantic City. When she returned my call, Kenny Bloom answered and was flabbergasted. He exclaimed, "Diana Ross is on the phone!" I took the call and asked Diana if I could escort her to Atlantic City. I knew she loved shooting craps.

She said, "I can't go there. People would mob me."

I told her to take Diana Ross off, put her hair up in pigtails, and come have some fun. She accepted my invitation, and after the show that night, we headed for Resorts International. We had a ball, and the beat went on.

We were escorted that night by the Spider Men, six skinny, gay, black, French martial artists who traveled with Diana. I called them the Spider Men, because these shadowy figures would always be crawling around within the audience, patrolling for anything that might be considered a threat to Diana.

One night we were working in a theatre-in-the round, and I was watching Diana perform. She was onstage singing a ballad when something happened that the Spider Men didn't see. But I saw it, and so did everyone in the audience.

While Diana was singing, a young man walked up behind her onstage with a butcher knife in his hand! The Spider Men crawled down and surrounded the stage. When the audience gasped, Diana turned and saw the man holding the knife. Then Diana did what she always seemed to do when encountering something that might be a threat. She simply walked up and put her arms around the young man and gave him a hug. The hug disarmed the young man both psychologically and physically, and the butcher knife fell to the stage floor. The dazed young man turned and walked off the stage, at which point the Spider Men grabbed him and made him disappear.

For the first time I will, out of respect, refer to her as Miss Ross.

The next tour was with Andy Williams. My tours with The Average White Band, Earth Wind and Fire, Blood Sweat and Tears, and Graham Central Station paled in comparison to the Andy Williams tour. The Andy Williams tour was to be the wildest tour I would ever experience. His relationship with the Kennedys and the "Camelot" image was not who Andy Williams really was.

In those days it was customary to play pranks on closing night. On one such night in Redwood City, California, I drove to a nearby farm and bought a goat. I put it in the back seat of my rental car and drove to the theater. When no one was looking, I let the goat loose in Andy William's dressing room. The next thing I heard was breaking glass. The goat had seen his own reflection in a mirror and had attacked it. Andy arrived at the theater to find his dressing room in shambles. His only remark was, "Thanks for the goat!" He told me it would make a great addition to his ranch in Colorado.

One night I asked Mr. Williams what it was like to be a star. He told me that he once was booked to perform at the Olympics in Munich, Germany. They picked him up from the airport with his companion a young lady and his art consultant, Billy Pierson, in a Mercedes 600 stretch limousine. They were taken to the newest and finest hotel in Munich. The hotel checked them into the wedding suite! Everything in the room was white. It was white, on white, in white, over white, and the background was white. Everything was white! Do you sense a perfect storm?

Billy Pierson went out to check on something and while he was gone, Andy and the young lady were chatting. Andy asked her if she noticed anything interesting about Billy Pierson. She said that she had not, and Andy pressed on.

"Doesn't Billy look an awful lot like Clarabell the Clown?" he asked her. He was bald on the top of his head and had bushy, curly hair around the sides and back.

The girl said, "Well, now that you mention it, Billy does look like Clarabell the Clown." Andy told her that there was only one problem. Clarabell had bright-red hair. With that, the plan was hatched.

Andy Williams called down to the bell captain and ordered bright-red hair dye. When it was delivered to the suite, Andy and the girl began preparing the dye for Billy's hair.

When Billy returned, they pounced on him and, despite his protestations, began applying the red color to his hair and eyebrows. Billy broke free, bolted into a bathroom, and locked the door.

By this time, the white-in-white-on-white suite was completely spattered with red hair dye.

Andy and the girl then tried to coax Billy out of the bathroom by kneeling near the bathroom door and slipping saucers of champagne under it. "Come out, Billy!" they taunted and then pulled the saucers back so Billy couldn't get them.

At this point, there was someone pounding on the door of the suite. The young girl answered the door to find the hotel manager, the hotel detective, and two Munich police officers, who barged into the suite. The hotel manager protested about all the noise and that his other guests were complaining. He asked what they were doing.

Andy Williams, still crouching by the bathroom door, turned and said, "We must get my friend Billy Pierson out of the bathroom so we can finish dyeing his hair red."

When Andy turned around, the police officers immediately recognized him, and one of the policemen yelled, "Billy! You must come out!" They didn't say a word about the red dye all over the suite. When the men left, Andy and the young lady immediately pounced on Billy and finished the job.

Andy then called down to the desk and informed the clerk that he did not like his suite. He requested to be moved, and within half an hour, Andy, the young lady, and Clarabell were moved to a fresh suite. That's what it's like to be a star.

The Andy Williams tour was fueled by cocaine. Never before had I experienced anything like it. It was everywhere. The power and image of Andy Williams allowed him to get away with murder.

One day we were working at an outdoor venue in Hawaii. During the show, Andy spotted a pretty girl in the audience. After the show, he sent an emissary out to invite her backstage. Her name was Miss Right. Andy told her that he thought he should bring her to Hollywood with him. Miss Right replied that he would have to ask her parents. Andy asked her where she lived, and she told him her home was on the other side of the island. Andy said, "Let's go visit them," and off they went in his limousine.

When they arrived, he walked her up the path to the modest home and knocked on the screen door of their porch. When the young girl's parents answered the door, Andy said, "Good evening. I'm Andy Williams, and I would like to take your daughter to Hollywood with me."

Her mother, not wanting to seem like a pushover, declared, "Well, we'll have to pack her things."

Andy went back to the limousine and waited. About fifteen minutes later, the eighteen-year-old Miss Right and her parents came walking down the path carrying all of the girl's possessions, and Andy's driver helped them put her belongings in the trunk.

When you're a star, people do not say no!

WILLIAM HENRY COSBY JR.

I've worked with Bill Cosby many times and he was always kind to me. I would watch every one of his shows and he was a true master. Sometimes we would have dinner together after the shows and I would joke with him by asking him to rate the show he had done from 1 to ten, ten being best. He would smile, but never answer.

Of course it was easier to have a comic open his shows because there was no band or piano to deal with, simply show up, do the show and move on.

I learned a lot watching him work. He would walk out with no introduction, sit on a stool and begin to speak with no set up. Now, my wife, he would say and then he would go on doing a bit on his wife. Bill Cosby would kill every show and I was flattered that he seemed to like my work and would ask me to be a guest when he would host *The Tonight Show*.

During my time with Mr. Cosby I never saw him with a woman nor did he ever talk about women. What he allegedly did later I cannot speak on, but there was gossip about him being a ladies man. I never saw that part of him!

I would gladly work with him again, but there are others who I would never work with again because of their behavior!

GOING IT ALONE

My first gig was at Harrah's in Reno, Nevada. Mr. Harrah would visit my dressing room on every opening night at his casino and chat with me. He once told me a story. There was a monthly board meeting with Mr. Harrah and all of the casino heads: the food and beverage manager; the hotel manager; the head maid; the casino boss; the head bartender; the executive chef; the bell captain; and the head of PR.

They all, in turn, told him the same thing. They told him he needed to raise the cost of drinks by twenty-five cents. He listened to them patiently, and after about an hour, he stood and said, "Ladies and gentlemen, thank you for all of your comments. I have learned that not one of you knows the business I am in. The price of our drinks will remain the same. You see, we are not in the drink-selling business. We are in the gambling business, and I will expect all of your resignations on my desk first thing in the morning!"

In the end he didn't fire these people, but his point was made, and they never again suggested anything like that.

This story inspired a routine that I did every night in his showroom: "Ladies and gentlemen, we love you here at Harrah's. Look at you. Look at you! We love you, and why wouldn't we? You, ladies and gentlemen, bring us your money, and you pay your own airfare to do it!"

When I did this, the audience rolled with laughter at the irony I had presented them with.

Then I got a call from my agent. He said that Soupy Sales' son had been hurt in an auto accident, and I was going to fill in for him at the Hyatt Regency in Detroit. The gig went on without a hitch and was especially fun, because I had the use of a full orchestra for the entire week. That's when I started doing encores.

During my stint in Detroit, I got a visit from the owner of a comedy club. At that time there were not many comedy clubs in existence. He wanted to have me appear at his club. I told him to contact my manager, which he did, and they worked out a deal. I began headlining at this new kind of club.

These comedy clubs were generally run by sole owners who had never run a nightclub before, and they had no idea what they were doing. I arrived in a town and went straight to the club to do my sound check. Not only had they never heard of a sound check, but they were also clueless about things like lights, sound, and how to seat an audience. When you seat a nightclub, it is customary to seat parties of two in front, parties of four behind them, and any party larger than that toward the rear of the room. This facilitates crowd control. The larger the party, the more likely they are to cause trouble by showing off for each other.

When I arrived for my sound check, I would also be confronted with a basketful of other problems. No lights, no sound system, and tables that were too large for the room. All these things were important to the show, and more than a few times I found myself at a hardware or furniture store with the club owner, buying the bare necessities needed to do a show.

There were also problems with audiences who had never seen a comedian perform in person. To this day, only fifteen percent of our population has ever seen a live show of any kind, let alone a comedian. They talked during the show, interrupted the show, and were ignorant as to how to behave during a show.

Also, the waitstaff had no idea what to do. They approached a table and screamed at the customers to take their drink orders. The liquor was also a problem. The emcees told the audience to drink up because the show would be better that way. This is a widespread misconception and is an insult to me. Drunk audiences are the worst. I know liquor is a necessary evil and is part of the club owners' profit stream, but it has to be handled with some savvy.

These problems were universal at comedy clubs, and I had to train every club owner in the country on how to properly run their clubs so they could generate more revenue. In other words, I had become an unwitting trailblazer!

I was walking along the Santa Monica Pier when I noticed a little shack in which a gypsy fortune-teller was sitting. On a lark, I went in and sat down. She read my palm and told me that I was going to make a lot of money in the music business. I considered this to be silly but paid her and left. I would soon find out that she was telling me the truth, even though I had never considered music as an option. I would soon be doing just that!

I was selling out every club I worked, and thanks to the shrewd deals my manager negotiated, I was the most active stand-up comedian, this without ever having a TV series. The sheer number of TV appearances I was doing, over 1,700 network and syndicated appearances, and counting, in my career was more than enough to fill every seat, in every room, on every night. The club owners also made more money than they ever had or would when I appeared. Yes, there were stars making more in situation comedies, but it wasn't from stand-up comedy.

MAKE ME LAUGH

I was in a market one night when a lady who was familiar with my work stopped me. She was working on a show called *Make Me Laugh* and said I should go in and talk to the producer, George Foster. It sounded like a show that pitted comedians against one another, and I was not enthusiastic about the proposition. But after some consideration, I decided to take the meeting.

I liked George Foster right off. He told me about the show. Each contestant faced three comedians in turn, and they would have sixty seconds to make the contestant laugh. I liked the idea. Because of my background, I asked him if he expected me to be a monologist on his show. He said that he would put no constraints on me, and I could do anything I wanted to, within the boundaries of Standards and Practices. I took his offer.

Well, *Make Me Laugh* was the best thing that ever happened to me. The show was a sensation and was wonderful for my career. I thought I was becoming well-known for the TV I had done before *Make Me Laugh*. Then I realized that I had only been scratching the surface. Now I really couldn't leave the house!

George Foster was a wonderful man and was extremely supportive of me. If I did something on the show that went particularly well, he would come over to me during a break, grab both of my ears, pull me close, and kiss me on the lips! I was in Heaven. God Bless George Foster.

Make Me Laugh aired opposite the news twice a night, five nights a week, and it chewed up mountains of material. Even though the show had writers, the writers didn't do anything but drink beer and snort cocaine all day. They were of no use to me. So I doubled my efforts and began to write even more than I was already writing. This was possible because I had no limitations on what I could write and would do anything. I didn't have the luxury of being fussy about what I did. I had to try every idea I had. Some of the bits that I didn't think were strong turned out to be the best ideas I had.

Nothing I had previously done, including *The Tonight Show*, had the impact of *Make Me Laugh*. I couldn't go anywhere without being mobbed by fans, and this was not enjoyable to me. I found myself embarrassed by the constant attention and would avoid going out in public. I did 517 episodes of *Make Me Laugh*, and a woman even named her first child Addotta Campbell after me!

After three seasons, the wonderful host of our show, Bobby Van, died of brain cancer. Two weeks later our producer, George Foster, died of the same thing. The show did not survive this double blow. "Addotta Brings Lyricism into the Art of Comedy"

PORTLAND OR. FEBRUARY 6, 1988

"Unlike a lot of comedians making the rounds these days, Kip Addotta approaches his art with many of the instincts of a musician or poet.

"It's perhaps appropriate then that Addotta will be performing here at 9 p.m. Saturday at the Starry Night music hall at 8 N.W. Sixth Ave., at least his third Portland engagement in as many years.

"In a telephone interview, Addotta agreed that he put quite a bit of forethought into his material.

'Some nights I do some improvisation, but it gives a whole new meaning to the word,' he said, laughing.

"Addotta's way with words has filled four comedy albums, several of them quite musical in presentation. And while he modestly agreed that, for a comedian, he had sold quite a lot of vinyl, he suggested it was not so much an attempt to make money as it was useful in building and maintaining a following.

"He did say he'd be doing a few musical pieces at Starry Night to the accompaniment of something he'd recorded for a portable sound system, though without the pair of dancing girls that had graced some past appearances.

"Addotta seems to write each of his pieces word by word, twisting clichés and incorporating outrageous notions that nevertheless come across in context, ranging from the humorously cynical to the disarmingly silly.

"It was Addotta who penned 'I Saw Daddy Kissing Santa Claus,' which threatens to become a Christmas classic.

"In performance Addotta is casual or conversational in manner, but he carefully times and enunciates his delivery, allowing an audience to keep up with his train of thought until it rolls right over them.

"Despite his forays into music, Addotta understands that he's a comic first and a musician only for laughs.

"As he has explained to audiences before, 'I used to wonder what kind of people would spend their time and money to watch comedy. Then I realized that you people can't dance.'

"But after more than 15 years writing and performing for everything from Johnny Carson's 'Tonight Show' to the big Las Vegas nightclubs, it's still impossible to predict what Addotta will come up with next, except that it will be funny."

COCAINE

I can't stress enough the amount of cocaine that was on the streets between 1975 and 1987, but it was good cocaine, not the poison they serve up today. It didn't matter where you went or who you were with, cocaine was everywhere. If cocaine was offered to you and you didn't accept it, you were considered an outsider who could not be trusted.

It seemed that everyone was holding. Doctors, lawyers, and even priests were holding. I know because I was there.

In Atlanta, Georgia, for instance, there was a disco and dinner house called The Platinum Club. At this club, there was a man and a women at the bar every night. He was a tall, lanky, cowboy type, and she was a pretty, young brunette. Everyone knew they were the go-to people in Atlanta. This went on for about five years, and then the couple announced that they were leaving town and wanted to throw a thank-you party for all of their "clients."

Their clients included the crème de la crème of Atlanta; doctors, lawyers, sports figures, politicians and even clergy. The party was thrown at the finest restaurant in Atlanta, Pano's and Paul's. On the evening of the party, at least 500 people showed up wearing their best finery. With everyone seated, the waiters locked the doors and pulled out shotguns. They announced, "FBI! Everyone is under arrest!" There was a queue of paddy wagons outside as far as the eye could see, and these luminaries were loaded up and carried to jail. It was, and remains, the largest drug bust in FBI history.

It was against the law, but cocaine really wasn't doing damage to anyone's health. Then the government got involved. They came up with the idea that if they outlawed the sale of ether used in the process of washing cocaine there would be no more cocaine problems.

Unable to purchase ether, the drug lords simply switched over to kerosene or gasoline to wash the cocaine. The result was that people started dropping dead, people like Pistol Pete Maravich and other sports players and ignorant citizens.

Finally, law enforcement began cracking down on the sale of cocaine. A Frank Sinatra was celebrating his fiftieth anniversary in show business, and the powers that be had ordered a lot of cocaine for the party. The supplier was a tall, silver-haired man named Simon. He had a pilot's license and would fly his plane down to Mexico and fly back with several kilos at a time. Several ounces of cocaine were delivered to the event's production company. The delivery method was simple. Simon would leave the drugs in his unlocked mailbox. Next, he would let the mule know where the drugs were. The mule would collect the product and leave money behind to pay for it. What Simon didn't know was that the police had been following this mule and had photographed the entire process. The mule was arrested. So was the owner of the mailbox, Simon. Simon, charged with possession of illegal drugs with the intention of selling them, was looking at stiff prison time. The judge declared that Simon was not read his Miranda Rights, and all charges were dropped. Simon was a free man.

As he walked past the arresting officer on his way out of the courtroom, Simon leaned over and said, "Go to hell." The detective threw Simon up against the wall and frisked him. And what did he find? A one-eighth-ounce packet of cocaine. Simon went away for four years! And how do I know all this? Because Simon lived next door to a man I knew, and I saw Simon once in a while.

Fast forward... One day my phone rang. It was a man who was the designated cocaine dealer on the set of a movie. He asked me if I knew the words to "I'm in the Mood for Love. I lied and said yes. He told me to report to the set of *Bound for Glory* at the Ambassador Hotel where the Coconut Grove was located. I went and the crew put me into makeup and costume. In about forty minutes the director, Hal Ashby, put me through seven takes and had what he needed. The star of the movie, David Carradine came over to me and said, "I believe you," which was a high compliment coming from such a great actor.

THE DEATH OF MY FATHER

In 1992 I got a call from my cousin Vito Addotta in Rockford, Illinois, informing me that my dad had died. Luckily I was available and got on a plane to settle my dad's affairs. I checked into my cousin Joyce's house, threw my things into her spare bedroom, and then drove to my dad's home. Entering his home was cathartic. The smell brought back memories.

Of course, I went through his things. In doing this, I came across a black-and-white photograph of my mother and father engaging in sex. For all I know, it was the moment I was conceived. She was lying on her back; he was mounting her. The photo had obviously been set up by my father using a Polaroid Land Camera with a timer on it. He had posed my mother, set the timer on the camera, joined her, and there they were, she looking at the camera over his left shoulder, and he looking back at the camera. She was smiling, and he wore a familiar smirk.

This was the first photo I had ever seen of my mother. I sat at his kitchen table and studied the photo for the longest time. I had no prurient interest in this picture, only the interest of seeing my mother's face. Then, I set the corner of the picture aflame with my lighter, dropped it in an ashtray, and watched it burn.

LIVE FROM MAXIMUM SECURITY

In 1989 I was a man with a plan. I wanted to take a production crew into a maximum security prison and do a concert for the inmates.

My producer, Reggie Fisher, and I went to prisons all over the State of California. We paused our search at one of the most notorious state prisons in the world.

San Quentin State Prison, California's oldest and best-known correctional institution, was established on the site currently known as Point San Quentin. San Quentin was, and is, an intimidating location in every sense. It was old, big, bad, and wonderful! The warden was interested in our idea, so we went to see him and the place several times.

Each time we went to the horror that is San Quentin, we were required to sign a hostage agreement, which stated that if taken hostage, no inmate would be released in order to spare our life. This, in itself, made our sphincters tighten! The warden gave us several tours of the facility and, I must say, familiarity did not make the place any less creepy.

During our negotiations we saw every nook and cranny of this sprawling dungeon of a long-gone era, including Death Row. The paint was peeling, and the walls seeped moisture which ran down to the floors in a never-ending waterfall. The inmates were dark, shadowy figures who mumbled and screamed at will. San Quentin was a noisy place, and a mere visit to this frightening location could make any criminal change his ways and follow the straight and narrow. I stopped driving over the speed limit, just in case.

At one point the warden asked us how much we wanted to be paid for this concert. I wisely said, "Nothing," wanting to avoid the paperwork and scrutiny that I knew would ensue. The deal was done, and we set a date for one month later.

We began to prepare for this adventure. A crew had to be gathered, and background checks were run on everyone who would enter the facility. Trucks, recording equipment, and cameras had to be rented, and rehearsals had to be done. As the date grew nearer, we all began to wonder if we had bitten off more than we could chew. I also brought along my backup singers, Lauren Adams and V. Paterson, aka The Bitches.

We arrived at San Quentin before sunup. Serious men came out and began the rigorous task of searching every crate, box, purse, pocket, and sleeve. Hostage agreements were signed, and when the gate finally opened with a clank and a groan, we all knew there was no turning back. We pulled onto the grounds, and two sets of gates closed behind us. We were in the slammer!

We slowly rolled over to the auditorium, and the crew began to load in. The Bitches and I were escorted to the dressing room area and got into our stage clothes. The ladies and I went over our notes. We had one shot at this, and I had no intention of making even one small mistake.

When the riggers, the camera crew, and the sound engineers were ready, and before the inmates were escorted in, we did sound and light checks. Nothing was left to chance. The three of us went backstage and began putting the final touches on our hair and makeup. We could hear the men filing in. They were loud and talking and joking with one another and were 2,000 strong. The inmates who were on lock-down, like Charlie Manson, were not allowed to attend. Thank God! I knew Charlie would have tried to do something that would draw all the attention to him, and I did *not* need that.

Showtime arrived and the inmates were not to be kept waiting. This was a treat for them and one could both hear and feel the anticipation coming from them. I sent The Bitches out first, and they took their place at their mic. Of course the inmates erupted into catcalls and whistles. My producer and I were backstage, waiting and listening for the men to settle. It took about ten minutes for this to happen. I gave Reggie the nod, and he went out to begin the music for my entrance.

I stood alone in the dark wing, waiting for the music to arrive at my walk-on cue. Precisely on the downbeat, I put my best foot forward and walked out. Prison guards were on the floor and lining the stage between us and the audience. At this point, a great calm came over me, and I went into committed-mode. I walked to center stage and was given a reasonable reception. I paused and waited for the men to settle again. This was it!

When the room became completely silent, I said, "Good evening, ladies and gentlemen!" When they heard this and realized that I was paying respect and showing some knowledge of life in the joint, they exploded into cheers out of returned respect for me. It was all I could do to keep from bursting into tears.

"Addotta Shoots from the Hip, Hits Bull's-Eye"

By Larry Kart of the Chicago Tribune

"Today almost every young stand-up comic wants to be thought of as both funny and hip-if only because he knows that he is speaking to people who have come to believe that if something is both funny and hip, the act of laughing at it will make them hip, too.

"But Kip Addotta, who is at Zanies through Sunday, doesn't play that game. Instead, like Lenny Bruce, like the early Rodney Dangerfield, like Shecky Greene to some extent, like several generations of musicians and shingles-and-siding salesmen, Addotta seems to be a genuine hipster—a man whose vision of life was always askew, not a guy who has cooked up a set of attitudes that he thinks might be cute.

"Actually, at 43, Addotta is almost a generation younger than any other hipster comic who comes to mind. But he has all the traits—the most crucial, for my taste, being the sense that everything he says arises from some reservoir of private experience, which he is willing to share with the audience but which he also is determined to husband and protect.

"That is, while Addotta knows that he is up there to sell his jokes-just as those salesmen know that their job is to hustle siding, and the dance-band tenor saxophonist knows that before the night is over he's going to have to play 'Misty'—he sells those jokes in such a way that he, and we, know that he's selling them.

"Now there's a hip way to do that, which was popularized by Steve Martin and is currently practiced each weeknight by David Letterman—an ironically coy and cool distancing of oneself from the very idea of joke-telling, not to mention the whole climate of show business.

"But the hipster style, which Addotta embodies, is quite different. Hot rather than cool, it wholeheartedly embraces the greasy contradictions of the entertainer's role-insisting that there is no way to forget that show business is still a business, no matter how much one might want to dance away from that uncomfortable fact.

"So in the area of honesty, Addotta has a running head start. And his graceful, rather deliberately paced and slightly sing-song delivery adds to the air of conviction that helps him sell his stuff.

"When, for example, Addotta says, 'Never snicker at the judge,' one is fairly sure that he once did just that and lived to regret it. And even though it's unlikely that the next two jokes in that particular string are based on personal experience ('Never go up to the Queen of England and say, "How much?"' and 'Never pick a stranger's scab.'), somehow they too feel real.

"Much of what Addotta says can't be printed here, so you'll have to trust me that most of it is very funny and very different from what most of today's young comics have to offer. Certainly his line about those self-righteous citizens who have one ashtray in the house and it's shaped like a lung.

"It's hard to believe that the same guy who made famous a song called 'I Saw Daddy Kissing Santa Claus' once intended to be a priest.

"But Kip Addotta says he actually spent two years in a seminary at the urging of his grandmother, before realizing that his true calling in life was comedy.

"The switch, he says, had less to do with vows of poverty and chastity, than with the fact that he was partial to sermons that elicit belly laughs.

"Released in 1986, 'Slaw Lane' follows detective Sam Spud investigating a murder committed on 'cucumber the first,' with the prime suspect being his own sister-in-law Peaches, 'a soiled but radishing beauty.'

"Peaches, it turns out, has been raisin cane at home, while sowing her wild oats with the no good Basil, a guy 'in a yam.'

"An irrigated Detective Spud eventually unpeels this mystery, after weeding out 'remaining' problems.

'Puns are not a major portion of my act, but they are very popular with the audience, especially with egg heads,' Mr. Addotta says, noting college students react best.

'Both "Life in the Slaw Lane" and "Wet Dream" took about six months each to write. "Wet Dream" was the first. I got the idea from a joke I did, which asked why is it that every time they catch a shark and cut it open, they find a license plate inside? Who are these people who drive into the ocean and park next to a shark?'"

"A sort of jack-of-all-trades comedian, Mr. Addotta prides himself on not letting puns or any other gimmick dominate his act. He may read poems one minute, launch into a monologue the next, then turn around and sing a song. Sometimes he just stands there and tells jokes. The variety may have hurt his career overall, he says, noting that a lot of popular comedians have made names for themselves for their insults, costumes and minority humor. 'I wasn't born in New York. I did not come from a poor family, and I'm not a member of a minority group. Talk about paying your dues,' he has been quoted as saying.

"Actually, Mr. Addotta is Italian, a fact which he says predetermined he would either be: A) a priest; or B) a barber. Because his grandmother had her heart set on option A, Mr. Addotta claims he was sheltered from the real world for most of his youth. When Grandma died, two years into his seminary training, Mr. Addotta decided to assert his independence. He then moved to option B.

"Mr. Addotta says he might still be working in a barber shop, had his wife not died. He was 25 at the time and had two children.

'Her death made me realize how short life can be. There's no such thing as security. It got me thinking I'd better do something with my life,' says the 44-year-old in a phone interview. 'There's nothing more pitiful than someone whose life ended before they'd done what they wanted to do. I look at this calling like a ministry. It has nothing to do with fame and fortune. I'm just expressing myself through comedy.'

"Mr. Addotta says he had been an amateur comedian since childhood, with a knack for clever turns of the language. When he finally got up enough nerve to prove his talents to the world, he packed up the youngsters and moved to Los Angeles.

"After suffering through three rough years, including a day job parking cars, he eventually hit it lucky working in the L.A. comedy club circuit.

"The big break came in 1974, when he was invited to make an appearance on the 'Tonight Show.' Though Mr. Addotta was terrified beyond belief at the time, Johnny Carson was impressed enough to invite him back. He has since been on the show 32 times. 'It's a very intimidating show,' Mr. Addotta says. 'They have this formula they seem to follow to make you feel intimidated, starting with not leaving the name of first-time guests at the front gate. They don't give you a dressing room, either.

'The second time you appear, they give you a dressing room in the basement. With each successive appearance, it gets a little better. Eventually, you end up with a dressing room upstairs, with a bathroom, telephone and television, if you're lucky. It's fascinating to me, because someone actually takes the time to work all that out.'

"'Everything Goes' was a game show that aired in the US from September 12, 1981 to September 28, 1988, with comedian Kip Addotta as host. It originally aired on Escapade for its first three years, then moved to the Playboy Channel in 1984.

"Addotta is the perfect host for "Everything Goes" because he has a quick, dry wit that contrasts with the show's wild, glitzy style. 'I must say, I did say something clever on one of those shows,' he deadpanned when asked to recall some funny moments. 'As I think back on it, it was rather clever. This girl put her bare breasts through these holes in what was called the Reveal Board, and I said to the audience, "Imagine those in a tight sweater!"'

He laughed at his own joke, then said, 'Most of the good stuff comes off the top of your head, I think. I quit writing things down, other than crib notes, a long, long time ago.'

"Addotta first gained national attention on 'Make Me Laugh,' the 1970s game show now in syndication.

'I really found myself on that show,' he recalled. 'That show wiped away any leftover fear that I might have had of appearing on camera. That's when I finally became a journeyman.'

"Since then, Addotta has pursued his career differently from most comedians. Rather than going the talk-show or situation-comedy route, he's concentrated on recordings. He's made three comedy albums containing music and monologues, and will start a fourth.

"He's even made a video for his latest comedy tune, which is called 'Wet Dream.' He described the song as 'an underwater comedy,' made up of puns about fish. 'They love it in Seattle,' he claimed. 'I understand they have a lot of fish up there.

'I'm not that computer-readout guy that can go on a television series,' he observed. 'I'm not that nice. I'm rather provocative. And the last thing we want to do on television is be provocative. We'd rather pander.'

"That 'genuine hipster,' Kip Addotta, will begin a five-night stint at The Punch Line Tuesday."

"Always a favorite with Columbia comedy fans, Addotta draws his material straight from real life. No market research or trendy fashion jokes from this guy -- just hilarious stories and one-liners delivered in a style that lets the audience identify with the storyteller.

'I try to speak their language, and I don't mean speaking with a drawl,' he said. 'I've traveled the entire English-speaking world and have a liberal education in human nature.'

"For more than 18 years, Addotta has crisscrossed the country, playing colleges and clubs. He's appeared on the 'Tonight Show' with Johnny Carson about thirty-two times and recorded two critically-lauded comedy albums, 'Comedian of the United States' and 'Life in the Slaw Lane.'

"Kip Addotta has the ability to make you like him right off. So when he takes the stage for an hour's worth of comedy, there is none of that initial uneasiness in which a comedian must prove himself to a skeptical crowd.

"You want to laugh, not just because you paid for a ticket, but because Addotta's cool, easygoing manner puts you in a nice, relaxed mood, as though you're sitting in someone's living room with that old college friend who could always get you laughing. That was the strategy he used on 'Make Me Laugh,' the syndicated show in which comedians tried to get contestants laughing before a timer went off. Addotta was the one who sauntered casually in and started a conversation and before the contestant knew it he or she was cracking up, without knowing exactly why.

"It worked on the show and it worked last night at the Richmond Comedy Club, where Addotta opened a four-night stint to help the club celebrate its fifth birthday.

"Addotta would follow strings of very funny but rather conventional jokes with a sort of subdued monologue that didn't seem to have any jokes in it, but somehow everybody in the place was laughing right along.

"At times, he paused for more than a breather, and it seemed as though he was searching for material. Whether he actually was, or whether this was simply part of his planned pacing, is of little consequence, for he always found what he was searching for and got the audience recharged.

"Sometimes he would stop an extended joke, gaze at the audience as if pondering some moral dilemma, then come up with some non sequitur such as, 'How do we really know they improve the taste of dog food?'

"Addotta took off after complicated diets, reducing all weight-gain problems to the simple notion that if you eat a lot of food, you get fat. 'If you eat a ton of celery, how much do you weigh? A ton.'"

To New Comics and Comedy Club Owners:

As you move along in your chosen profession with due diligence, you should become better and better at what you're doing. You learn the tricks of the trade, if you will. These are the little things that increase the entertainment dynamic of your performance. If you're a comedian, these little pieces of knowledge enable you to get bigger, longer, and better laughs from the audience, and have nothing to do with the jokes but with the effectiveness of the jokes.

Let's start with temperature. An audience that is warm will not laugh anywhere near as well as an audience that is cool. For comedy the room temperature should be at seventy degrees. When an audience is warm they become lethargic and sluggish and respond to a performer with little enthusiasm. You should know something about temperature in order to be most effective at what you're doing.

Here is the formula: Each person in the audience creates ninety BTUs of heat. In other words, each person creates the same amount of heat as ninety candles. So, if you have an audience of, let's say, two hundred people, they will create 18,000 BTUs of heat, 18,000 candles. And this is not taking into consideration the heat generated by the stage lights, which can be another 500 to 10,000 BTUs. This is a possible total of 28,000 BTUs.

So, what is the solution? To keep an audience of 200 people at seventy degrees, the room's air-conditioning system must be at least 30,000 BTUs. This is a piece of information that all nightclub owners and performers should know in order to have good shows and make a good amount of money for both the club owner and the performer. If the club has this equipment in place everyone will enjoy the show, spend more money, and look forward to returning for another evening of entertainment.

Also, the air conditioning should be set at seventy degrees at least one hour before show time to bring the room's temperature down to the proper level before the audience begins to arrive. Now, at the beginning of seating you will get complaints generally from the ladies that the room is too cold. When a lady complains, the person she complains to should say, "We'll take care of it right away," and then do nothing at all. As the audience fills up, the temperature of the room will rise simply because of the body heat being generated by the increasing size of the audience. The lady will be happy, and the show will have an increased chance of being successful.

How to Seat a Showroom

Seating is important. Comedy club owners balk at this, because it requires staff and extra time and may cost them money. Club owners balk at anything that will cost them money. Even if it doesn't cost them money because they do it themselves, they will still balk because it will take effort. And none of them know the first thing about it anyway. Customers come in and the club owner or manager utters that infamous phrase, "Sit anywhere you want!" In that instant they have already ruined what could have been a great show.

Never, if you know what's good for you, allow "festival seating" when people are allowed to seat themselves. There is a formula to seating a showroom that has been handed down through the ages but has long been forgotten by most. Seating is the very essence of crowd control. Assuming that you have a crowd to control. However, if you don't do it properly you will never have a crowd to control in the first place!

Here is the formula: One must put a little "Reserved" card on every table. The reason for this is that the average schmo who comes to your show believes that sitting near the stage will put them in jeopardy of being picked on by the comedians.

I, personally, have never picked on an audience member, and why would I? These people have paid to see my show. Why would I make people uncomfortable after they have paid to see my show? I could never figure that one out. And people like me, Richard Pryor, Steve Martin, Steven Wright, and many others have never done it, and it should not be done. However, when the average schmoes hear the word comedy they always think they're going to be picked on by the comedian. That's what the "Reserved" signs are for. A showroom should always be seated using the following formula and there are no exceptions.

When the audience begins to arrive, you seat them in order of the size of their party. In many cases, when the seater says, "Right this way" and begins to lead a party to a table near the stage, one in the party may say, "Oh, we don't want to sit this close to the stage." The seater can say, "All of these tables are reserved." Then, pointing at the table where he wants to seat the party, the seater can say, "This table is reserved for you. Enjoy the show," and simply walk away.

This achieves two things. First, the party feels important, because they have a reserved table, whether they asked for one or not. Second, it places them at the table where we want them to sit. That's why it's called crowd control. The seater of the house must have and use authority when seating the audience. Remember, it's not up to the customers to choose their seats. It's up to the house, meaning us. If you have a seater who is shy and timid you lose control of the room immediately. The rule is, "polite, but firm."

Here is the seating formula: 1. Parties of one or two people are always seated closest to the stage; 2. Parties of four are seated behind them; 3. Parties of six are seated behind the parties of four; 4. Parties of more than six are always seated toward the rear of the room.

Why? Because the larger the group the more likely you are to have a heckler among them, because the schmo believes he has more power to behave badly when he's with a group. And, God forbid, they do cause trouble, possibly even to the extent of stopping the show. It's much easier to throw a group out of the back of the room than it is to extricate them from the front, in clear view of the rest of the audience. Remember, when it comes to a successful show, things that are done or not done before the show are much more effective than measures taken during the show. Everything must be done to ensure that the show is not hindered by the incompetence of the staff. Also remember that we have a responsibility to the people who have paid to see our show, to see that the event is not ruined by a few people who have been improperly seated.

Stage Lighting

Lighting on the comedy club stage is usually terrible, because the club owner doesn't want to spend the money. Surprise, surprise! The thing I notice about lighting on the stage is that it's too damn bright. Whoever is in charge doesn't know enough, or care enough, to adjust the stage lights properly and check them every night. It's too bad that I have to refer to the phrase "comedy club," because the fact is, these rules apply to all clubs and theaters.

However, comedy clubs are no different than any nightclub. There is a stage, there are tables and chairs, and they serve food and liquor. But over the years people have come to believe that comedians can only work in comedy clubs.

The lighting is important in any venue. After all, lighting creates the mood in the room.

The people who run nightclubs have evolved into nothing but cashiers who turn the lights on at the beginning of the night and off at the end of the night. Then they check out the registers, make notations on the money taken in that night, and go home.

Well, there's a lot more than that involved in running a successful business. When your product is entertainment of any kind, you must take care of all the little details, and all the details should be directed at making the show as effective as it can be.

As I mentioned earlier, I usually find that the lighting in showrooms is too bright. Lighting controls should be the slide type slide one up for brighter and down for dimmer. What actually happens is that whoever is in charge of the lights simply turns them all the way up at the beginning of the night and all the way down at the end of the night.

Well, there's a lot more involved in it than that. You see, stage lights are usually arranged and spread out horizontally across the ceiling in front of the stage, each set having a separate slide control. The lights to the far right and far left of the stage should be dimmer than the ones toward the center, so that the center of the stage is the focus of attention.

But even the lights at the center shouldn't be turned all the way up. When you have slide controls on the lighting system, there are a thousand different settings between all the way off and all the way on. Sadly, in today's world, most of the people in charge of these matters have no idea of this and simply turn the lights all the way up and go back to playing with their iPads. If the lights are all the way up, the entertainer or entertainers look pale and unhealthy, giving the audience the impression that the performers are not attractive and, therefore, not worth paying attention to. Looks are important! And the first round of drinks should have already been served at least ten minutes before showtime.

Also, there's the timing of the lights. In a showroom, the stage lights should be dimmed almost all the way down until five minutes before the show begins. Then, during that five minutes, the lights should be gradually brought up to performance levels. This serves to alert and draw the audience's attention to the fact that the show is about to begin, and they will adjust their chairs and focus their eyes and ears in the direction of the stage. Little things like this can have a tremendous effect on the audience's enjoyment of the show. It gives them the comfort and confidence of knowing that the staff of the club or theater knows what they're doing.

SOUND

If you're not early you're late! Believe it or not, sound is more important to a comedian than it is to a musician. Here's the reason for this: in music, the audience often already knows the words to the songs they're listening to. In comedy, the audience does not know the words to the routines and must now get this and be able to hear the difference between a B, a D, a K, a P, and a T.

In order to achieve this, one must have the sound system equalized in what is called "straight up and down," which means that you are neither adding to nor subtracting from the treble, upper mid-range, mid-range, or base. In other words, it means that when you speak, it sounds exactly like your true voice, with no, as we say, EQ.

From the audience's end, the sound must also seem like it is coming from the direction of the performer. We don't want the sound of the performer on stage to seem to be coming from the back of the room or the middle of the room. Why? The human ear is flared out at the back so we can tell which direction a sound is coming from. If the sound seems to be coming from any direction other than the performer, it is distracting and difficult to understand the words.

Many a good performance has been ruined merely because the audience didn't understand the words coming out of the performer's mouth.

And, if you're performing in a room for a week, the sound must be checked again before each evening's performances. Why? Because, and this goes on in every showroom in the world, the cleaning crew comes in after the shows, and what do they do in the wee hours of the morning after their cleaning is done? They get onstage and sing! Because they don't know how to sing, they go up to the sound booth and turn the base way up to make their singing sound better.

This problem can be solved during the original sound adjustment by putting strips of masking tape along the side of each soundboard slide and knob and marking the tape with lines to show where the volume levels are supposed to be and at what settings the equalizer knobs were placed. This makes rechecking the sound easy, because you can quickly reset the controls to the levels they were at before the cleaning crew changed them.

Remember, if you want to be a successful entertainer, there are no small matters. We all want to make money, you and I and the club or theater owner, so everything is important. It is taking care of the nuts and bolts before the first joke is told that enables the first joke to have a chance to work.

I never did hang around with other comics. I had nothing against them; it was mostly because I knew so few of them. With a wife and three children to support, I never had the time. As soon as I could find work, I took it. And work meant travel.

Even when I began to learn how to do this thing, I wouldn't do just one open mic each night; I would do five. I never had the time to hang around in front of places like The Comedy Store and talk shop with other comics.

Comedy isn't easy, and it takes all the concentration one can muster to learn how to do it. Everything in comedy must be considered. In comedy, no situation can be left to figure out later; it must be figured out before it happens.

For comedians who are starting out, I can offer some suggestions that may seem confusing until tried. Young comics I've been watching don't know what they're doing. They watch each other and then repeat the mistakes they've seen other comics make. It goes on and on and on.

Stage Craft

Everything I do on stage, I do from the perspective of the audience. Here is what should be done:

When new comics are on stage, they always seem to choke up and stand too close to the front lip of the stage. This forces the ringside audience to raise their heads up and back in order to see the performer's face, causing them great neck discomfort. Move the mic stand back three or four feet from the lip of the stage so that the audience members in front can lower their heads to a level position and be more comfortable.

Many beginners and so-called experienced comics counter by saying that they don't use the mic stand, choosing to hold the mic instead. This is also a mistake new comedians make and is made by almost every comic working today. Holding the mic in one's hand is a mistake, because, to an audience member, it looks an awful lot like a weapon, subliminally speaking. It makes the audience uneasy.

Do not "swallow" the mic. Believe me, the audience can hear you! Let the mic do its job and you do yours. How many times have you seen an award show and witnessed the recipients bend down to get closer to the mic. It makes them look awkward and breaks the audiences' eardrums. These are supposed to be experienced actors and musicians?

Another popular excuse I hear is that the performer holds the mic in their hand because they like to pace back and forth on the stage. If one wants to speak to the audience at stage left, simply step to the right of the mic and speak over the mic in that direction, and vice versa. This lets the audience members keep their heads in one position and is much less fatiguing for them. Think it through from the audiences' perspective and do everything from that viewpoint.

"But everyone holds the mic in their hand." No, they do not. Mick Jagger and rap artists do it, because they see so many people making this mistake and they copy it. When I see a performer holding the mic, gripping it so hard that their knuckles turn white, I know that this performer is scared to death. Not only that, but these same amateurs who intend to, someday, perform on TV will have a rude awakening when they walk out onto a studio stage and realize that there is no mic, but a boom mic instead, and they must contend with the problem of not knowing what to do with their hands.

Now let's talk about hands. Sammy Davis Jr. taught me that one should show the palms of ones hands upon mounting the stage. This sends a subliminal message to the audience, letting them know that you're not carrying a weapon and that you're not a threat. Everything I do on stage, I do from the audiences' point of view.

Another mistake I've seen many comedians make is asking questions. Comedy is about simple declarative statements.

Hecklers are not born; they are made. If you don't want hecklers, stop asking the audience questions. "How you doing? Are you having a good time? Anybody here do this or do that?"

Comics who do this are simply stalling for time, because they don't have enough material to fill their time slot. There is no question that can't be replaced with a simple declarative statement. "I'm glad to see you're enjoying the show," or "I'm feeling great." and so on and so forth. Try it; you'll like it!

Don't Curse

The language you use on stage is a reflection of who and what you are.

The way you speak to an audience defines the way the audience thinks you feel about them. If you choose to use four letter words and scatological references, the audience will know that you have no respect for them.

Toilet humor, or scatological humor, is a type of off-color humor dealing with defecation, urination, flatulence, and, to a lesser extent, vomiting and other bodily functions. It has seen a substantial crossover with sexual humor, such as penis and vagina jokes.

Remember, you are talking to strangers. If you were to walk up to a group of people you know and use this kind of language, they already know that you speak this way and will tolerate it, though they may have a generally low opinion of you. However, even if all your friends use this type of speech, they will respect you for not using it. It's up to you.

If you use it to an audience of people you don't know, they will see it as a sign of disrespect, even if they use such language in their private lives.

Furthermore, it's a lot more fun to use your vocabulary rather than take the lazy way out and use four-letter words. I can speak about the most intimate subjects in front of the most conservative audience and make it palatable to them, and they will enjoy my performance because of it.

When I'm writing it makes it a little more difficult, but using proper vocabulary makes the work more interesting to write and more interesting for the audience to listen to. Audiences know all the cuss words, but if you work without them, they'll appreciate your efforts and like you for it.

In addition, believe me when I tell you that when you craft a joke without the cuss words and it works, it feels wonderful and raises your self-esteem considerably. Self-respect is key to performing with confidence, and it pays you a lot more money.

And, of course, if you want to take advantage of lucrative corporate gigs, you'll be able to do so without making adjustments.

But what if you're following some idiot who uses a lot of profanity, and here you come along with clean material you're going to do in front of an audience that has been demoralized before you can get at them? As a headliner, I would have already spoken with the owner or promoter ahead of time and informed them that I do not want anyone in front of me who is a "cuss meister." If you're not the headliner, here's what you do. You follow the idiot on stage and you say, "Well, I can only hope that I can maintain the standard that has been set by the previous performer (idiot). Join me in a big round of applause for . . . fill in the blank (idiot). Then you applaud with the audience.

I stumbled onto this technique, and it has never failed to work. For some reason, it erases all the damage that the idiot has done, and you can then go on with a civil, well-mannered, killer show without the crutch of the cuss words and have a wonderful, if not great, set. Guaranteed!

Hecklers and the Rule of Three

Hecklers are not born; they are created, most of the time, by comedians who do not know what they're doing!

Also, in spite of what you've seen in movies, most hecklers are not men. They are women! In my forty-year career, I have had one male heckler. The rest were all females.

Why is this? When a man goes out for an evening of entertainment, he knows one thing: if he acts like a jerk he stands a good chance of getting punched in the nose. In general, women don't have to worry about this.

This is why, as I have mentioned before, it is very important that a comedian never ask a question of an audience, because you're liable to get an answer. Again, I have seen many so-called comedians make this mistake, and they can't seem to wait to make it. Usually it's the first thing out of their mouth. "How are you doing?" This is how hecklers are made.

"Common sense is not common practice." I have given this advice to many comedians just before they go on, and still the first thing out of their mouth is, "How are you doing?" The silly part of this is that the comedian doesn't want to know how the audience is doing. And yet they're bent on making this mistake every time they walk onto a stage. So, with the first words out of their mouths, they have lost control of the audience.

Again, there is never, ever, any reason to ask an audience a question. Comedy is about simple declarative statements, and all sorts of things can be used to open a set without asking a question. When you ask a question of an audience, you are likely to get an answer. You don't want that. I never do anything on stage that does not benefit me, and that includes asking a question.

Here comes "the rule of three." If you should have the misfortune of having a heckler, remember, they're wanting a reaction from you, bide your time. Let the first heckle go unnoticed and unanswered. If this heckler does it a second time, do the same thing. Go on with your show as if it didn't happen. After the second heckle from this person, the audience will become irritated by the heckler. If it happens a third time, you can go after them, but never in a mean way. Never try to top the heckler. If you do, the audience will revert to being on the heckler's side again. Remember, the audience sees you as the pro and does not want you picking on anyone, including the heckler. After the third heckle you have the audience on your side, so be careful how you respond.

Here is the way I'd respond. I'd say, "Madam (or Miss), you are interrupting our show." Notice that I do not say *my* show, but *our* show. This is done to further gather the audience to your side of the dilemma. "All of these people have paid their hard-earned money to see our show. You don't seem to be interested in seeing it, so if you want your money back, we'll give it to you and you may leave."

I guarantee that you will receive a resounding and supportive round of applause from the rest of the audience, and you won't hear another peep out of the heckler or anyone else the rest of the evening!

You see, an audience wants to know what is expected and what will and will not be tolerated from them. So often this is the first and only live show they've ever been to, and they have no experience being an audience member. They've seen movies and watched TV but never actually witnessed a live performance, and they do not know how to behave.

BECOMING A COMEDY PRO

Since it's likely that you have never actually seen a professional comedian before, I will give you some guidelines. But before I do, remember this: people who do open-mic nights know as much about performance as grasshoppers know about lawn mowers.

When you've done all the work and begin to get laughs, you have taken the first step to becoming a professional comedian. You can now begin to hone your style. Honing one's style is the process of becoming the special character that you are, naturally, a character unlike anyone else. Finding yourself is key to becoming a distinctive character, one the audience will identify only with you.

When one begins the journey to becoming a pro, it is natural to put on the guise of someone you admire. This should be a temporary thing to enable you to have the time to morph into who you really are.

The guises I used were David Brenner and Steve Martin. I would take on their style but use my original material. Gradually you will shed your guises and come out on the other end as yourself. This process took me about six years, until I had peeled off every last shred of my guises and became Kip Addotta. Once this stage is over, you'll find yourself in warp speed and grow at a remarkable rate.

You'll begin to get laughs with much more regularity. Your confidence will build, and you'll be on your way to becoming a Master Blaster, Zen Master of your craft.

I always audiotaped my shows, and, more important than that, I listened to the recordings the next day to further polish my presentation. With this hard work and attention to every detail, I was becoming a monster, in a good way, of course.

When I thought I was nearing perfection, which no one ever attains, I learned a harsh lesson on how much I didn't know. One night, in Atlanta, Georgia, I was performing in a nightclub. The place was packed with about 550 people, and I was rocking the house. I had a roll going that was like a ferocious storm at sea.

When listening to the recordings of my shows, I had been timing how much space was between each major laugh. My calculation told me I was getting a major laugh every eight seconds. I thought I was becoming state-of-the-art, and then the bottom fell out from beneath me!

I was rolling along that evening, and about an hour into the show, a man about eight feet from the lip of the stage was laughing so hard that he couldn't stop. This, of course, caused the rest of the audience to laugh even harder at the dilemma the man was in. Even I was laughing. Then, it happened. The man could not catch his breath, and he aspirated in his mask, fell to the floor, and died. Aspirating in your mask is when all the air in your body goes past your throat and you cannot get breath in.

Of course the audience was stunned; I was stunned. The man was dead!

I remember thinking to myself, *Well, I've already done an hour. There is nothing I could do to help this man, and I would never and could never bring the audience back into control. However, these people would never forget this show.* I backed away from the stage, hurried into my dressing room and out to my car, and drove back to my hotel. I was in shock.

So, what lesson had I learned? The lesson was that, like a jockey, I must learn to pace the audience in the same way a jockey paces a racehorse during a run around a track. From then on I would bring an audience to a certain level, and then I would back off and let them settle down before going on with my set. This is called pacing. And in order for me to learn this lesson, a man had to die.

So when a comic comes up to me and says, "I killed!" I think to myself, *No, you didn't, and I hope you never will.*

Plebs and Twerps

If I had a nickel for every time I've had someone say, "I'm a comedian too!" I would be a much richer man. When I started in the business of comedy, there were fifty comedians in the US. Do you know how many there are now? Fifty!

Going onstage at an open-mic night does not a comedian make. The terrible truth is that almost every one of these so-called comedians has never even seen a real comedian work. They watch each other work and copy the mistakes of the other wannabe comedians. They do not know how to walk on stage, deal with the mic, handle a crowd, or even begin a show.

Yes, I am angry. It's pitiful to watch these slime balls pretend to be comedians and go around telling people that they are comedians. Most so-called comedians are nothing but people twenty-nine years old and still living with their moms. They have given the art of comedy a bad name. People leave comedy shows today, saying comedy isn't funny. And they're right.

What they're doing is not comedy. It's the ramblings of people who haven't learned anything and will never be anything, because they do not have the courage to talk about their own feelings. They spew things that they've heard other people say.

DINNY

In 2000, I was sitting next to a statuesque redhead at the bar of Dan Tana's, my go-to bar in West Hollywood. I said hello, and she looked me up and down as if I were a bug. The same thing happened three times, but this lady would not talk to me! The next time I saw her, I said nothing at all. Then a woman came over to us and said, "I'm tired of this," and then went on to say, "Dinny, this is Kip. Kip, this is Dinny." It turned out that this lady would not speak to me, because she had not been formally introduced to me.

We then struck up a conversation, and we have been together ever since. Dinny is a wonderful watercolor artist and a great lady. This woman has put up with all of my eccentricities and has been my closest friend in every sense of the word. I have never met a woman who enjoys having a man as much as Dinny. This is for keeps!

Dinny is, however, intractable and feisty. She has a typhoon-like temper. If you cross her, the penalty will be delivered swiftly and without mercy.

On the other hand, Dinny is kind and generous and always takes great pleasure in pleasing me.

Dinny is also a traditional woman with an imperious demeanor. Similar to royalty. She never cusses or gossips. She is defensive about her friends, and woe be to the person who says anything negative about one of her pals.

She is gentle and dainty, except when it comes to electronics, which she treats like they were made of titanium. She believes that if one of the buttons on a remote control doesn't work, the solution is to press on it until her thumb goes completely through the dang contraption.

Considering all the people I have known, I have few friends. But the friends I do have are good and true. So, I guess I am ahead on this count too.

I fully believe that I will live for many more years, God willing.

I owe everything to my grandmother, Donna Chicca Francesca Addotta, who raised me, and I have faith that I will join her again someday. At first she will give me a good scolding for the mistakes I have made, and then she will take me in her arms, and, with a handkerchief that she will retrieve from her purse, she will wipe away all the little smudges on my face, and we will be together for eternity.

"In the end, it is not the shouts of your enemies you will remember, but the silence of your friends." I have found these words from Martin Luther King to be the most profound thing I have ever heard. It is the encapsulating, defining, reason for life itself. If you've ever wondered, What's it all about? now you know!

The best years of my life are yet to come. I have worked hard, settled my debts, and best of all, I like myself.

Liking one's self is the most important goal one can achieve. It takes much effort to be born, grow up, marry, raise children, and get to the stage of self-approval. If you do not like yourself, you still have work to do.

I have not and will not ever stop learning. However, I have that lesson well-studied. Of course, many people engage in self-loathing. They are correct in doing so. Who else would know better than they if they have not been good, decent people? Psychiatrists try to get people to stop loathing themselves. I disagree. People should go on disliking themselves until they prove to themselves that they have, indeed, earned the badge of self-esteem.

Again, I am nothing, if not imperfect, and in my imperfection, I am perfect! In nature there is nothing that runs in a straight line. As a matter of fact, in order to find sunken treasure or man-made objects, divers at the bottom of the sea look for anything containing a straight line.

They say that advice is the worst vice. Well, pardon me while I engage in the worst vice. Stop expecting perfection from yourself. Strive for it, sure; but know while doing so that you will never achieve it. Be happy with what God has given you and get rid of all your mirrors. Fire your tattoo artist and your piercer. You are imperfect! Please stay that way and have a good day.

Life is good!

In Conclusion

In the end, after some 1,737 appearances on network and syndicated TV, four top-ten records, and countless personal appearance tours, I must say that my most precious accomplishments have to do with my family.

I have raised three beautiful children who are good people and positive contributors to our society.

There is no more worthy accomplishment than being a good father and husband. My first child, Victor, is a great guy, a wonderful craftsman, and a good husband to his wife, Sibylle. My middle child, Kathy, is an admirable wife to her husband, Michael, and mother of my granddaughter Kayla. My youngest child, Frank, has overcome insurmountable challenges and has become a good husband and father of my other two granddaughters, Lauren and Sofie. All of my granddaughters are straight-A students. Frank and his wife, Deicy, are on their way to becoming Cordon Bleu chefs.

My first wife, Mary, was a loving mother and wife who gave me my first two children and then passed away due to kidney failure at the age of only twenty-three. However, my second wife, Lynn, took over and raised my first two children, along with one of our own, with extraordinary grace and love. I owe her a debt of gratitude that I will never be able to repay. She remains a great lady!

I am a blessed man. I say this knowing that I could have done better. I am nothing if not imperfect. As a man who traveled for a living, I fell for temptations that I wish I could have been man enough to resist. But, to my credit, I did resist many other temptations that came my way. I have never been involved with another man's wife or woman.

I have never stolen from anyone and seldom, to my own detriment, been a liar.

I have worked as hard as one can work at every endeavor I have ever taken on and continue to do so. What success I've had or will have is more from hard work than talent, although I thank God for the talents he has seen fit to endow me with.

I will go to God with a clear, if only slightly soiled, conscience.

Made in the USA
Lexington, KY
05 May 2018